AMERICAN POLITICAL, ECONOMIC AND SECURITY ISSUES

VOTING ALTERNATIVES, HOTLINES AND WEBSITES

AMERICAN POLITICAL, ECONOMIC AND SECURITY ISSUES

Additional books in this series can be found on Nova's website
under the Series tab.

Additional E-books in this series can be found on Nova's website
under the E-books tab.

AMERICAN POLITICAL, ECONOMIC AND SECURITY ISSUES

VOTING ALTERNATIVES, HOTLINES AND WEBSITES

SEAN M. THOMAS
AND
DANIEL P. ALLTON
EDITORS

Nova Science Publishers, Inc.
New York

Copyright © 2011 by Nova Science Publishers, Inc.

All rights reserved. No part of this book may be reproduced, stored in a retrieval system or transmitted in any form or by any means: electronic, electrostatic, magnetic, tape, mechanical photocopying, recording or otherwise without the written permission of the Publisher.

For permission to use material from this book please contact us:
Telephone 631-231-7269; Fax 631-231-8175
Web Site: http://www.novapublishers.com

NOTICE TO THE READER

The Publisher has taken reasonable care in the preparation of this book, but makes no expressed or implied warranty of any kind and assumes no responsibility for any errors or omissions. No liability is assumed for incidental or consequential damages in connection with or arising out of information contained in this book. The Publisher shall not be liable for any special, consequential, or exemplary damages resulting, in whole or in part, from the readers' use of, or reliance upon, this material. Any parts of this book based on government reports are so indicated and copyright is claimed for those parts to the extent applicable to compilations of such works.

Independent verification should be sought for any data, advice or recommendations contained in this book. In addition, no responsibility is assumed by the publisher for any injury and/or damage to persons or property arising from any methods, products, instructions, ideas or otherwise contained in this publication.

This publication is designed to provide accurate and authoritative information with regard to the subject matter covered herein. It is sold with the clear understanding that the Publisher is not engaged in rendering legal or any other professional services. If legal or any other expert assistance is required, the services of a competent person should be sought. FROM A DECLARATION OF PARTICIPANTS JOINTLY ADOPTED BY A COMMITTEE OF THE AMERICAN BAR ASSOCIATION AND A COMMITTEE OF PUBLISHERS.

Additional color graphics may be available in the e-book version of this book.

Library of Congress Cataloging-in-Publication Data

Voting alternatives, hotlines, and websites / editors, Sean M. Thomas and Daniel P. Allton.
    p. cm.
 Includes index.
 ISBN 978-1-61324-593-4 (hardcover)
 1. Voting--United States. 2. Federal Voting Assistance Program (U.S.) I. Thomas, Sean M. II. Allton, Daniel P.
 JK1976.V65 2011
 324.6'50973--dc22

               2011014556

Published by Nova Science Publishers, Inc. † New York

CONTENTS

Preface		**vii**
Chapter 1	Alternative Voting Methods September 2008 *U.S. Election Assistance Commission*	**1**
Chapter 2	Voter Hotline Study *U.S. Election Assistance Commission*	**63**
Chapter 3	Voter Information Websites Study *U.S. Election Assistance Commission*	**113**
Index		**149**

PREFACE

This book provides details about new and exciting ways of administering elections so that each jurisdiction can chart the future of its own system of election administration with the most information possible. States and localities will need to evaluate their own processes before any change in election administration is advisable. Alternative voting methods discussed are changing the date of the Federal Election Day, instituting a uniform poll closing time, and voter hotlines and websites.

Chapter 1- The U.S. Election Assistance Commission (EAC) is an independent, bipartisan commission created by the Help America Vote Act (HAVA) of 2002 to assist State and local election officials with the administration of Federal elections.[1] The EAC provides assistance by disbursing, administering, and auditing Federal funds for States to implement HAVA requirements; conducting studies and other activities to promote the effective administration of Federal elections; and serving as a source of information regarding election administration.

Chapter 2- The telephone remains a primary communication tool between election offices and the customers they serve—America's voters. Election officials nationwide use a variety of tools to provide information to stakeholders. From answering routine questions on Election Day to providing poll worker training and assignment information and responding to inquiries on the status of provisional ballots and general voter complaints and concerns, the outcome of this study reiterates the importance of providing fast, efficient, and accurate election information.

Chapter 3- In interviews with election officials and the information technology (IT) professionals working for election jurisdictions, some distinct patterns emerged in the development of voter information websites. Projects that were developed with dedicated time and thoughtful consideration stood out. Likewise, projects that came together as add-ons to existing sites rarely received high marks. Many of the projects at the focus of this study were created as a result of use of the Internet and associated technologies in daily operations. The development of computerized voter registration lists and the software to maintain them, removed the barrier to creating a database that a Voter Information website can query.

In: Voting Alternatives, Hotlines and Websites
Editors: Sean M. Thomas, and Daniel P. Allton

ISBN: 978-1-61324-593-4
© 2011 Nova Science Publishers, Inc.

Chapter 1

ALTERNATIVE VOTING METHODS SEPTEMBER 2008

U.S. Election Assistance Commission

EXECUTIVE SUMMARY

The U.S. Election Assistance Commission (EAC) is an independent, bipartisan commission created by the Help America Vote Act (HAVA) of 2002 to assist State and local election officials with the administration of Federal elections.[1] The EAC provides assistance by disbursing, administering, and auditing Federal funds for States to implement HAVA requirements; conducting studies and other activities to promote the effective administration of Federal elections; and serving as a source of information regarding election administration.

Section 241 (b)(10) of HAVA requires the EAC to study "[t]he feasibility and advisability of conducting elections for Federal office on different days, at different places, and during different hours, including the advisability of establishing a uniform poll closing time and establishing – (A) a legal public holiday under section 6103 of title 5, United States Code, as the date on which general elections for Federal office are held; (B) the Tuesday next after the 1st Monday in November, in every even numbered year, as a legal public holiday under such section; (C) a date other than the Tuesday next after the 1st Monday in November, in every even numbered year as the date on which general elections for Federal office are held; and (D) any data described in subparagraph (D) as a legal public holiday under such section."[2]

In 2006, the EAC commissioned two studies about alternative voting methods currently used in the United States. One study involved a national survey of voters regarding their opinions on matters such as changing the date of the Federal Election Day, instituting a uniform poll closing time, and increasing confidence in the voting system, among many others. The other study resulted in this publication, *Alternative Voting Methods*, which examines the experiences of selected States and/or local jurisdictions with voting outside the traditional precinct-based polling place through early voting, vote-by-mail, and vote centers. Sections in this publication address the feasibility and advisability of conducting Election

Day on a different day through weekend voting and declaring Election Day holidays. The final section reviews voting in Puerto Rico.

The Alternative Voting Methods *study is meant to provide details about new and exciting ways of administering elections so that each jurisdiction can chart the future of its own system of election administration with the most information possible.*

Each alternative voting method in this report is feasible in nearly every State because the changes to current election administration practices mostly require legislation at the local, State, and/or Federal level. Not every method would be successful in every jurisdiction, however, nor would every jurisdiction be able to handle the costs of implementing each alternative voting method. The *Alternative Voting Methods* study is meant to provide details about new and exciting ways of administering elections so that each jurisdiction can chart the future of its own system of election administration with the most information possible. States and localities will need to evaluate their own processes before any change in election administration is advisable.

EARLY VOTING IN TEXAS

Early voting is traditionally defined as a process by which voters cast their ballots before Election Day at precinct-like polling stations throughout a jurisdiction. It requires no excuse from voters and is "virtually like voting on Election Day." The use of early voting has expanded throughout the country over the past several election cycles. Texas has been administering early voting for more than 20 years, making it a good choice for a case study into the alternative early voting method.

Texas began to implement early voting in 1987, although the process was somewhat different from the early voting of today. At that time, absentee voting was expanded to provide the opportunity to all voters to cast a ballot before Election Day. Counties were required to offer "absentee voting in-person" to all voters at any one of their permanent election office branch locations. In 1991, Texas State law was changed to provide a minimum standard for the number of early voting locations incorporated within each county. The law also permitted the creation of temporary branch locations for the express purpose of conducting early voting.[3]

In Texas, registered voters may vote at any early voting location within their county between 4 and 17 days before Election Day. If the 17th day before a Federal general election falls on a weekend, Texas State law requires that the start of early voting occur on the first business day thereafter for an overall early voting period of 12 days.[4]

Early voting procedures are similar to those already conducted on Election Day. Officials' clear procedures and forward planning has led to the success of early voting as supported by data showing an increasing proportion of voters that chooses to vote early. This section will provide information about the evolution of early voting in Texas by detailing the legislative history, reviewing the logistical issues surrounding the implementation of early voting, and examining the overall effect of early voting in the State of Texas.

State Name:	Texas
Chief Election official:	Hon. Roger Williams
	Texas Sec. of State
	Elections Division
	P.o. Box 12060
	Austin, TX 78711-2060
Total Number of Registered Voters:	13,074,279 (in 2006)
Alternative Voting Method used:	Early Voting
implemented:	1987

A thorough study about how early voting is administered in Texas from the perspective of election officials has not occurred to date. With the limited amount of source material available, this case study was conducted using statutory references, personal interviews, and published statistics from the Texas Secretary of State's office.

Implementation and Effect

Although voter participation data suggest that early voting does not increase overall turnout, election officials interviewed have seen clear benefits. An increasing percentage of voters take advantage of early voting with each successive Federal election. For local election officials, the lighter volume of voters on Election Day equates to shorter lines, fewer complaints, and a more efficient Election Day environment.

No empirical studies are available regarding election officials' attitudes about early voting, but anecdotal evidence from throughout Texas suggests that it was greeted with general reluctance, which was to be expected with any unfunded mandate. More than 20 years after implementation, however, local election officials have fully incorporated any extra costs associated with early voting into their budgets and reported that they favor the alternative voting method.

Since its inception in 1987, early voting in Texas has undergone significant changes to address matters pertaining to equal protection, accessibility, and inconsistencies within the Texas Election Code (TEC). All these changes put early voting practices and procedures on par with those used on Election Day.

LEGISLATIVE HISTORY

1987

Texas House bill 612 is enacted, which creates "no-excuse" voting by personal appearance. Voters no longer need to provide a reason if they wish to vote in person before

Election Day. Only a limited number of early voting locations are established, however, usually in the permanent branch offices of the county election official. Moreover, the State and local officials do not lead an aggressive public education effort to inform voters of the new alternative voting method. Local election officials are especially nervous about paying for the new form of voting for which the State provides no funding.

1988

The Committee on Elections of the Texas House of Representatives reviews the implementation of expanded absentee voting. It seems as if the new option is well received by both the general public and the local election officials implementing and administering it. Included in the committee's report are the following findings:

- The success of the expanded in-person absentee voting program is reflected in an increase in the number of absentee votes cast, which encourages the creation of more in- person absentee voting locations.
- The concerns about the ability of voters to cast more than one ballot during the early voting period appear unfounded; no data suggest that multiple voting occurs.[5]

MAJOR MILESTONES IN THE EVOLUTION OF EARLY VOTING IN THE STATE OF TEXAS

1988: The State of Texas permits no- excuse, in-person absentee voting.

1991: Requirements mandate early voting locations in counties with a population of at least 100,000 residents, expanded hours— including on weekends—for early voting, procedures, and noticing requirements. State law recognizes early voting as a distinct form of voting.

1993: Early voting legislation becomes effective statewide; all counties must establish temporary (early voting) branch locations beginning up to 20 days before an election.

1997: The Texas Legislature further defines the quantity and distribution of early voting locations in counties with populations of more than 120,000 and less than 400,000. the early voting period is shortened to 17 days before an election.

2003: All counties are required to begin early voting 17 days before an election.

These findings prove to be an impetus for subsequent changes to the TEC. One improvement is the adoption of technology and procedures- such as real-time connectivity between early voting sites and the central office poll book- meant to mitigate the threat of multiple voting.

1991

On May 26, 1991, Governor Ann Richards signs Senate bill 1234, which revolutionizes voting in Texas. The law amends the TEC to identify "early voting" as a separate and distinct voting method apart from "absentee voting." Among the substantive changes are rules that require the following:

- Clerks' offices must remain open on Election Day.
- Counties with more than 100,000 residents must establish temporary branch early voting locations, open early voting polling places 12 hours each day during the final week of early voting, and observe extended hours during the last weekend of early voting.
- Electioneering must take place outside larger boundaries near early voting locations to put procedures in line with Election Day electioneering.
- Clerks' offices must establish uniform voting hours for all early voting locations.[6]

The 1991 legislation calls for an early voting period beginning 20 days before the election. Subsequent amendments narrow the early voting period to provide greater uniformity in the voting process. Today, the current period of early voting begins on the 17th day before a general election or the first business day thereafter if the 17th day before the election falls on the weekend.

ESTABLISHING EARLY VOTING LOCATIONS

Early voting sites are not chosen at random. State law defines the formula for establishing early voting locations for State and Federal elections as follows:

- Counties with populations of less than 100,000 are required to maintain early voting locations at the main office of the county election official and any permanent branch locations.
- Counties with populations between 100,000 and 120,000 are required to maintain one early voting location within each County Commissioner District if the county receives a request from within a particular precinct by 15 or more registered voters.
- Counties with populations between 120,000 and 400,000 are required to maintain one early voting location within each County Commissioner District plus a main early voting location (minimum of five locations).
- Counties with populations of more than 400,000 are required to maintain one early voting location within each State Representative District plus the main early voting location.
- The total number of permanent branch and temporary branch early voting locations in one County Commissioner District may not exceed twice the number of permanent and temporary polling places open at that time in another County Commissioner District.[7]

The County Commissioners Court, the governing body of each county, is the ultimate authority for the placement and use of early voting locations throughout the county. All decisions about the placement of early voting locations must be official actions of the court, which are posted on the agenda of their regular meetings. Furthermore, there are statutory requirements to ensure that the placement of early voting sites is fair and politically neutral.[8]

The current statutory requirement for the relatively equal distribution of early voting locations among County Commissioner Districts (not to exceed a ratio of 2:1) provides a valuable tool for maintaining a minimum level of equality in service because each County Commissioner District is required by law to have roughly the same population.

Although each county must achieve minimum compliance with the law, many pursue additional alternative methods allowable under the TEC. Some counties have established "mobile early voting" locations. These locations are open for limited durations and are intended to serve particular areas. All mobile locations are subject to the same noticing requirements and procedures as stationary early voting buildings.[9]

COSTS

Texas has not conducted a statewide review of the costs associated with early voting. Tarrant County, however, the third largest county in the State and home to the city of Fort Worth, estimates that the direct costs associated with conducting early voting during the Presidential election in November 2004 amounted to $524,320; more than 57 percent of that expenditure is attributable to payroll and the hiring of additional clerks.

Tarrant County establishes 28 early voting locations for the duration of the early voting period and an additional 9 locations of limited duration. Because of its large population, Tarrant County is required to conduct early voting for a period of 12 hours per day (Monday through Friday) during the last week of early voting. During the 2004 general election, the county's 307,246 early votes cast averaged a cost of $1.70 per early voter according to interviews with the Tarrant County Elections Administrator.

In Harris County, the State's largest county, with 1.9 million registered voters, the cost per early voter in the 2004 Presidential election was $1.14. Total costs associated with the 32 early voting locations in Harris County totaled $471,073, and an estimated 72 percent of that amount was for personnel expenses, according to interviews with the Harris County Clerk.

Other costs associated with early voting include telecommunication line installations, site rental fees, and transportation fees to transport voting equipment to and from early voting locations. The cost per early voter varies from election to election based on the level of turnout during early voting.

Personnel Costs

Payroll expenses account for a substantial percentage of the money required to conduct early voting in Tarrant and Harris Counties. To conduct "Election Day" over an extended period, local election officials must hire temporary employees, who are paid at a higher pay rate than that of standard Election Day poll workers.

In 2007, supervisors at an early voting location in Harris County earned $8.49 per hour, while election clerks earned $7.92 per hour. Election Day poll workers in Harris County earned $7.50 and $6.00 per hour, respectively, for the equivalent positions.

Technology Costs

With many early voting locations open and processing voters simultaneously, counties use modems and other telecommunication devices that provide real-time connectivity to the elections office to prevent multiple voting. The need for this technology was first identified when Texas expanded no-excuse absentee voting. At that time, the Texas Legislature wanted to ensure that voters could cast only one ballot during each election.

Early voting requires using off-the-shelf or internally developed election management software. The software offers a user-friendly interface for processing voters by election clerks while verifying a voter's registration status. The voter is then given credit for voting. After given credit, the individual is unable to vote in another early voting location or on Election Day. Should this connectivity be lost for some reason during voting, emergency procedures are in place to verify voters via telephone so that no voters are turned away from an early voting location. The increased telecommunication requirement adds to the costs associated with early voting—approximately $4,600 in Harris County, for example.

ADMINISTRATIVE CHALLENGES

The public expects reliable early voting each election, and local election officials continue to improve administrative practices and procedures to meet those expectations.

Counties are considering ways to inform the public during early voting about which sites are experiencing long lines and how best to redirect voters to alternate locations. Officials continue to examine the potential for more early voting locations and how best to rapidly verify a voter's eligibility, because the ability to process voters quickly is critical to the success of early voting in any jurisdiction.

Harris County has started using Geographic Information System software to analyze voter trends within service areas, identify gaps in service coverage, and anticipate the potential effect of moving early voting locations.

VOTER TURNOUT

The Texas Legislature initially justified its approval of early voting with a supposition that providing greater ease and flexibility might yield higher turnout. Early voting is certainly more convenient for voters; sites are open for many more hours during the course of the election cycle than they would be if voting occurred only on Election Day. The voter makes the decision of when and where to vote based on his or her schedule. Early voting, however, appears to serve only as an alternative voting method for active voters who would have otherwise voted on Election Day. Overall turnout as a percentage of registered voters has not increased, so little evidence supports the supposition that large proportions of previously nonvoting individuals are now participating because of the convenience provided by early voting. It is possible, though, that convenience is keeping some voters in the process that might otherwise have stopped voting without the alternative voting option.

Figure 1 illustrates the traditional ebb and flow of turnout associated with Federal elections. Presidential election years are usually the highest turnout elections. In Texas, the most noticeable trend in the data is the dropoff that occurred between the 1992 and 1996 Presidential elections—from a high of more than 70 percent in 1992 to 53 percent in 1996.[10] Although 2004 showed a slight increase in turnout, the overall trend since early voting began reveals no dramatic increase in turnout. Instead, it has remained relatively stable at slightly more than 50 percent during recent Presidential election cycles.

Figure 2 illustrates the increasing proportion of overall voting in Texas that occurs during early voting. Although the level of overall turnout has remained the same, the percentage of those voters choosing to vote early continues to grow when similar elections are compared. In 2004, the proportion of early voters of overall turnout was more than 50 percent for the first time. One trend of particular note is the double-digit increase in the percentage of early voters from 2000 to 2004. Future elections will reveal whether the trend continues.

Figure 3 shows the daily turnout for the 15 most populous counties in Texas in the 2-week early voting period before Election Day. During the first week, early voting is limited to the 8-hour workday. During the second week of early voting, hours are extended to 12 hours per day in each of the 15 counties. The data show that for both the 2004 and 2006 general elections, a dramatic increase in turnout correlates with the expanded service hours during the second week of early voting. Local election officials should consider these data when implementing an early voting process. If 2 weeks of early voting proves too expensive, the same convenience voting effect may still be achieved in 1 week of early voting, because it appears that most voters decide to vote as close as possible to Election Day.

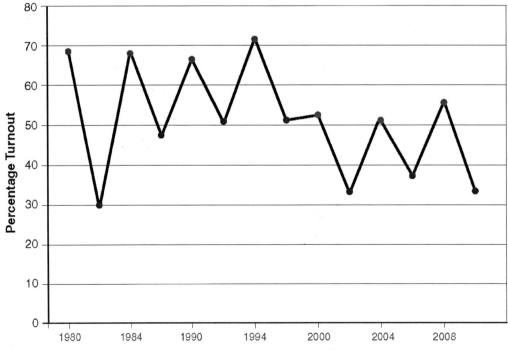

Source: Texas Secretary of State, Elections Division, Election Results Archive, 2006.

Figure 1. Overall Turnout (RV) for Federal General Elections (1980–2006).

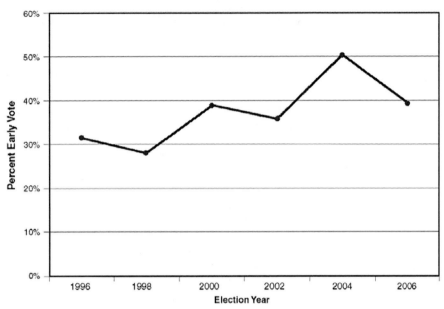

Source: Texas Secretary of State, Elections Division, Election Results Archive, 2006.

Figure 2. Early Voting as a Percentage of Overall Turnout.

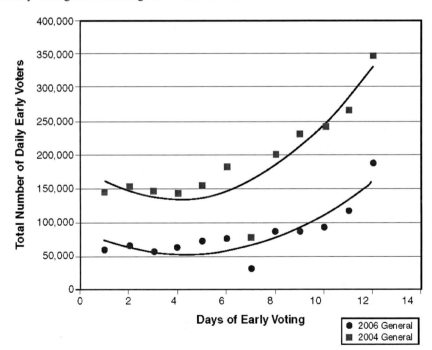

Source: Texas Secretary of State, Elections Division, Election Results Archive, 2006.
*Day 6 represents a Saturday—the first voting day with 12 hours of voting. Day 7 represents a Sunday, with limited voting hours in many counties, which results in far fewer votes than the immediately preceding and succeeding days of early voting. Days 8–12 represent the second week of early voting, with 12 hours of voting each day.

Figure 3. Daily Distribution of Early Voters 2006 versus 2004 General Elections*.

LEGAL CHALLENGES

Texas won its first early voting legal battle when the 5th U.S. Circuit Court of Appeals ruled that "because the election of federal officials in Texas is not decided until Texas voters go to the polls on federal election day, we conclude that the Texas early- voting scheme is not inconsistent with federal election laws."[11]

In 2003, the Mexican American Legal Defense and Education Fund (MALDEF) sued Bexar County (TX) election officials.[12] The election involved in this dispute was the Texas State Constitutional Amendment election scheduled for September 13, 2003. Because of low turnout expectations for this election, the number of early voting locations was decreased from the number used on a typical Federal Election Day. MALDEF claimed that the reduction of early voting locations happened in particular demographic areas that would be more likely to deny equal access for voters of some minority groups. The U.S. District Court ruled that the county had not properly secured preclearance through the U.S. Department of Justice under Section 5 of the Federal Voting Rights Act, which is required in some jurisdictions before changing an election practice.[13] In addition, the overall distribution and existing levels of access of early voting locations were deemed insufficient. Bexar County was required to establish an additional six early voting locations.[14]

In an effort to alleviate questions of equal access, the TEC now defines certain noticing provisions to registered voters regarding the schedule and locations for early voting. Any changes to early voting schedules or early voting locations must be submitted for Section 5 preclearance through the U.S. Department of Justice, as required by the Federal Voting Rights Act.[15]

CONCLUSION

The success of early voting in Texas can be attributed to its statutory foundation, distinct rules that establish minimum service requirements for voters, and defined operating procedures for local election officials. Key portions in the TEC and best practices used by election officials include the following:

- Clear rules for the uniform application of early voting hours and dates.
- Unambiguous minimum and maximum requirements for the quantity and distribution of early voting locations to ensure equal access within a county.
- Noticing provisions that inform the voting public about early voting locations, dates, and times and also inform them of any changes.
- Detailed procedures for processing voters during the early voting period.
- Technology that permits real-time connectivity for verifying early voters.

As the popularity of early voting increases, so does the number of challenges for election officials. They must periodically reassess early voting service areas within their jurisdictions. As demand for early voting in one area increases, officials must respond by identifying and planning for new early voting locations as needed.

Despite the fact that early voting has not increased overall turnout in Texas, as was originally hoped, it has been embraced by both the public and election officials. Voters have the flexibility of choosing a convenient time and place to cast their ballots- something they may be unable or unwilling to do on Election Day- and long lines at polling places and resulting consequences become less likely for local election officials on Election Day. Continued increases in the proportion of the electorate choosing to use early voting signal that the alternative voting method has become an integral part of the election process by voters in Texas.

ELECTION DAY AS A HOLIDAY: ILLINOIS AND MARYLAND

In a national survey of voters conducted for EAC, 51 percent of individuals favored establishing an Election Day Federal holiday compared with 45 percent who opposed it. Many believe that an Election Day Federal holiday would result in more convenience for working individuals, which would result in higher turnout. There may also be some benefits for local election officials in the administration of elections on a holiday as opposed to on a regular Tuesday workday.

An Election Day holiday would not be new to voters in all States. As of 2006, nine States observed State holidays on Federal Election Days. The nine States are Delaware, Hawaii, Illinois, Indiana, Louisiana, Maryland, Montana, New Jersey, and West Virginia.[16]

EAC researchers interviewed State and local election officials in Illinois and Maryland, States with Election Day State holidays on Federal Election Days, for this section. Aside from collecting information about the pros and cons in administering elections on Election Day holidays, researchers gathered data about whether election officials believe that the holiday adds value to the election process as a whole—for election officials and voters.

IMPLEMENTATION AND EFFECT

Assessing the effect of implementing an Election Day State holiday in Illinois and Maryland is difficult because of a lack of information. In Illinois, the State declared an Election Day holiday in 1943. In Maryland, Federal elections have been State holidays since 1882. Election officials in each State were unsure of the reasoning behind the statute, how long it took to implement the statute, and how costly the statute was to implement.

State Name:	**Illinois**
Chief Election Official:	Dan White
	Executive Director
	Illinois State Board of Elections
	1020 S. Spring Street
	Springfield, IL 62704
	Phone: 217-782-1542
Number of Registered Voters:	7,320,000 (in 2006)
Implemented:	1943

State Name:	**Maryland**
Chief Election Official:	Linda Lamone
	Admin. of Elections
	151 West St. Ste 200
	P.O. Box 6486
	Annapolis, MD 21401
Number of Registered Voters:	3,142,812 (in 2006)
Date Implemented:	1882

One of the most common arguments in favor of establishing an Election Day Federal holiday is that it would become significantly easier for individuals who must work on Election Day to vote. In 1992, then-Representative Ron Wyden from Oregon said, regarding H.R. 3681 Democracy Day Act, "one of the largest barriers to voting is the busy daily schedule of the American people. The demands of home, work and family life often make it extraordinarily difficult to find the time to make it to the polls to vote."[17]

It is not clear, however, that an Election Day Federal holiday would necessarily result in a more convenient voting experience for voters. In States with Election Day State holidays, the U.S. Postal Service and all other Federal agencies remain open. Many businesses choose not to close. In some States, including Maryland, the local jurisdictions determine whether schools, libraries, and other municipal buildings will be open as usual. In short, a State holiday guarantees the closing of only State offices. The same would be true of an Election Day Federal holiday; the only guaranteed closures would be for Federal agencies.

The closing of State offices has some benefits for local election officials. Some jurisdictions recruit State employees to be poll workers for Federal elections on their days off. An Election Day State holiday may result in more options for local election officials in establishing polling places. Some States reported that more schools are available as polling places when is the State declares an Election Day State holiday. Again, an Election Day Federal holiday would not mandate that schools or State offices close, so the potential effect of such a holiday is difficult to measure.

Additional costs are associated with establishing an Election Day holiday. The States that have declared Election Day State holidays must pay for the loss of 1 day's productivity for all State employees. The same would be true if the Federal government were to declare a Federal holiday. More than 2.4 million Federal employees would be given the day off with pay.[18] Total payroll cost for poll workers is not likely to rise dramatically just because the Election Day is a holiday. Local election officials and their staffs already receive overtime pay or compensatory time because of the long hours they work on Election Day.

VOTER TURNOUT

Most arguments in favor of declaring an Election Day Federal holiday include an expected increase in voter convenience so that more individuals can participate in the electoral process. EAC researchers were able to identify data for Illinois regarding the number of votes cast for President in 1940 and 1944 as well as population estimates of voting age population (VAP). Similar data about the implementation of an Election Day State holiday in

Maryland were impossible to locate because Census Bureau data about VAP are not available before 1940.

In 1940, the last Presidential election before Illinois moved to an Election Day State holiday, 4,217,935 votes were cast for Presidential electors.[19] In Illinois, the civilian population age 21 and over (the legal voting age at the time) was 5,374,143.[20] Thus, the turnout of VAP in 1940 was 78.5 percent. Four years later, after the implementation in 1943 of the Election Day State holiday, votes cast by civilians for Presidential electors decreased to 3,873,805 out of 4,998,000 individuals in the VAP.[21] Therefore, turnout decreased slightly to 77.5 percent in 1944 after the implementation of the Election Day State holiday.

EAC researchers compared turnout data from the past four Federal elections in Illinois and Maryland and the 7 additional States that have Election Day State holidays with the aggregated turnout data of the 41 States and the District of Columbia that do not have State holidays and to the national voter turnout. The data are included in Table 1. In Federal elections from 2000 and 2006, the aggregated turnout of States with Election Day State holidays was higher in two elections and lower in two elections than the turnout of the 41 States and the District of Columbia that do not have State holidays. For example, in 2000 the 9 States with Election Day State holidays had a turnout of VAP of 50.6 percent while the national turnout was 50.0 percent. In 2006, however, the 9 States had a turnout of 35.8 percent when the national turnout was 37.0 percent.

Table 1. Turnout in Election Day State Holiday States, 2000, 2002, 2004, and 2006[22]

2000 Presidential Election			
State	**VAP***	**Voters**	**Turnout (%)**
Delaware	596,389	327,529	54.9
Hawaii	921,695	367,951	39.9
Illinois	9,218,881	4,742,123	51.4
Indiana	4,522,034	2,182,295	48.3
Louisiana	3,258,261	1,765,656	54.2
Maryland	3,974,596	2,025,480	51.0
Montana	678,630	410,986	60.6
New Jersey	6,359,586	3,187,226	50.1
W. Virginia	1,406,441	648,124	46.1
9 States w/ Election Day Holiday	**30,936,513**	**15,657,370**	**50.6**
41 States + Dc without Election Day Holiday	**179,783,669**	**89,718,116**	49.9
United States	**210,720,182**	**105,375,486**	50.0
2002 Presidential Election			
Delaware	613,468	232,314	37.9
Hawaii	950,627	382,110	40.2
Illinois	9,375,151	3,538,883	37.7
Indiana	4,569,767	1,521,353	33.3
Louisiana	3,298,931	1,246,333	37.8

Table 1. (Continued)

State	VAP*	Voters	Turnout (%)
Maryland	4,095,794	1,704,560	41.6
Montana	695,012	331,321	47.7
New Jersey	6,473,660	2,112,604	32.6
W. Virginia	1,414,041	436,183	30.8
9 States w/ Election Day Holiday	**31,486,451**	**11,505,661**	**36.5**
41 States + Dc without Election Day Holiday	**184,520,406**	**66,867,802**	**36.2**
United States	**216,006,857**	**78,381,943**	**36.3**
2004 Presidential Election			
Delaware	629,012	375,190	59.6
Hawaii	980,145	429,013	43.8
Illinois	9,518,511	5,274,322	55.4
Indiana	4,635,693	2,468,002	53.2
Louisiana	3,358,475	1,943,106	57.9
Maryland	4,200,864	2,386,705	56.8
Montana	715,516	450,445	63.0
New Jersey	6,573,016	3,611,691	54.9
W. Virginia	1,430,277	755,887	52.8
9 States w/ Election Day Holiday	**32,041,509**	**17,694,361**	**55.2**
41 States + Dc without Election Day Holiday	**189,243,590**	**104,600,617**	**55.3**
United States	**221,285,099**	**122,294,978**	**55.3**
2006 Midterm Election			
Delaware	650,932	254,099	39.0
Hawaii	991,442	344,315	34.7
Illinois	9,648,191	3,486,671	36.1
Indiana	4,758,146	1,666,922	35.0
Louisiana	3,138,364	902,498	28.8
Maryland	4,274,452	1,788,316	41.8
Montana	725,487	406,505	56.0
New Jersey	6,661,588	2,250,070	33.8
W. Virginia	1,427,746	459,884	32.2
9 States w/ Election Day Holiday	**32,276,347**	**11,559,280**	**35.8**
41 States + Dc without Election Day Holiday	**194,294,076**	**72,231,623**	**37.2**
United States	**226,570,423**	**83,771,171**	**37.0**

*VAP = voting age population

When the turnout data from States with Election Day State holidays are compared with the turnout data from States without Election Day holidays and with the entire country, it is evident that an Election Day holiday does not increase voter turnout.

ELECTION DAY IN ILLINOIS

The Illinois State Board of Elections was created in 1974, but the Election Day State holiday was implemented 31 years earlier in 1943. The Board of Elections was unable to provide information about how long it took to implement the holiday or any costs involved with the implementation. Similarly, it could not comment about changes in the administration of elections in Illinois as a result of the implementation of the Election Day State holiday. EAC researchers interviewed local election officials in seven jurisdictions in Illinois: Champaign, DuPage, Jackson, Lake, Mason, Peoria, and Rock Island Counties.

The Election Day State holiday is not advertised. As one election official explained it, the holiday has "been around for so long that people just take it for granted." Still, as only a State holiday, the U.S. Postal Service and other Federal agencies remain open during the day as do many private businesses. Assessing whether those private businesses might be more likely to close on an Election Day Federal holiday is not feasible.

ADMINISTRATIVE CHALLENGES

Illinois has a State law that requires all government buildings be made available to local election officials as polling places on Election Day. Local election officials, however, say they have had difficulty enforcing the law. Some school administrators are reluctant to allow their facilities to be used as polling places on Election Day because of security concerns for their students. The problem became more severe after September 11, 2001.

In Illinois, the decision to close schools on the Election Day State holiday is made at the county level. All seven counties represented in this study indicated that schools are open during the Election Day State holiday, which makes it difficult for local election officials to use those facilities. In addition, most of the counties cited parking problems at polling places located at open schools.

ILLINOIS LAW: (10 ILL. COMP. STAT. 5/17-25 2008)

5/17-25. Election days to be holidays: The days upon which the general elections for members of the House of representatives of this State shall hereafter be held shall be holidays, and shall for all purposes whatever as regards the presenting for payment or acceptance and of protesting and giving notice of the dishonor of bills of exchange, bank checks and promissory notes and as regards days of grace upon commercial paper, be treated and considered as is the first day of the week, commonly called Sunday; provided, that no other election day shall be treated and considered as a holiday.

The increased availability of State and local government buildings on the Election Day State holiday does not necessarily provide local election officials with greater polling place options. Although State government buildings are closed, the consensus among local election officials in Illinois is that government buildings are not ideal polling sites. Many government buildings have space configurations that do not provide enough room for polling places. An election official from a county that has used a State government building as a polling place noted that it is more difficult to gain access to the building during holidays because the regular maintenance and security personnel are not on site.

Most election officials interviewed told EAC researchers that there was no increase in interest in becoming a poll worker simply because State employees have the day off. Only one election official from the seven jurisdictions in Illinois interviewed for this case study indicated that the jurisdiction was able to recruit State employees as poll workers as a direct result of the Election Day State holiday.

The administrative cost to run elections varies by county. Five of the seven county election officials interviewed told EAC researchers that local election officials in the jurisdiction get paid overtime. Those election officials, however, receive overtime pay because they work more than the standard business hours on that day and not because of the State holiday. Costs would increase if the county government were closed for the holiday, which would mean the local election official and staff would receive either overtime pay or compensatory time off for working on the State holiday.

Possibly the biggest administrative benefit of an Election Day State holiday for local election officials is a side effect of the State closure unrelated to the actual administration of elections. County clerks are the election administrators in Illinois. Those clerks' offices are closed because of the Election Day State holiday, and local election officials can focus their offices' efforts solely on the election in progress. Election officials use other personnel from the clerks' offices to help with election administration, as needed.

Voter Turnout

All seven county representatives whom the EAC interviewed agreed that the Election Day State holiday in Illinois does not result in higher voter turnout.

The turnout data of VAP in Illinois verify the election officials' beliefs that turnout in their State is not necessarily higher than it is in States without an Election Day State holiday. In 2000, 2002, and 2004, voter turnout in Illinois was slightly higher than voter turnout nationwide. In 2006, however, voter turnout in Illinois was about 1 percent lower than national turnout.

ELECTION DAY IN MARYLAND

Election Day in Maryland has been a State holiday since 1882. Officials from the Maryland State Board of Elections were unable to provide EAC researchers information about the implementation of the holiday. Specifically, they did not know about the costs involved or how initial implementation affected voter turnout. EAC researchers interviewed local election officials in eight counties in Maryland: Allegany, Anne Arundel, Baltimore, Calvert, Carroll, Harford, Montgomery, and Washington Counties.

In Maryland, a State holiday requires the closure of only State government buildings. Counties, municipalities, and private businesses do not necessarily have to close because of the State holiday. Some counties and municipalities in Maryland have declared Election Day a county or municipal holiday but others have not.

Similarly, each school district has the authority to establish holidays in its jurisdiction. During the 2006 election cycle, 22 of the 24 school districts were closed for the primary and general elections. For jurisdictions in which schools are closed, local election officials attempt to make use of those facilities as polling places because they are generally accessible for voters with disabilities and have adequate parking.

Administrative Challenges

Schools are closed on Election Day in all of the eight counties that participated in this case study. In Carroll County, 32 of 33 polling places are in schools. In Montgomery County, 600 to 700 high school students work on Election Day at polling places, either as poll workers or helping in other ways during busy hours early in the morning and later in the evening. Election officials in a smaller jurisdiction also prefer using the closed schools as polling places.

> The first statutory reference to Election Day as a legal holiday in Maryland was in 1882. chapter 23 of the laws of Maryland (1882) designated "all days of general and congressional elections throughout the State" as legal holidays. the law related to presenting for payment or acceptance of bills of exchange, bank checks, drafts, and promissory notes on the designated legal holidays.

Election officials interviewed from all eight counties say they have more poll workers when State offices are closed. In Harford County, for example, 15 to 20 percent of the 800 poll workers are State employees who have the day off. In 2006, Maryland Governor Robert Ehrlich used an incentive to recruit State employees to use their Election Day State holidays to serve as poll workers. Although State law provides 8 hours of administrative leave for State employees in addition to poll worker compensation on days during which the employees are normally scheduled to work, the Election Day State holiday for Federal elections renders the State employees ineligible to receive the administrative leave because they are not scheduled to work. In a September 22, 2006, letter to all State employees, the Governor declared all State employees eligible for the administrative leave in addition to the poll worker compensation irrespective of the State holiday.

Voter Turnout

Maryland has had a higher voter turnout rate than the national voter turnout rate in each of the last four Federal elections. During the 2002 and 2006 midterm Federal elections, Maryland recorded between 4.8 and 5.3 percent higher turnout than the national voter turnout rate. In fact, of States with Election Day State holidays, only Montana had consistently higher voter turnout rates than Maryland. This consistently higher turnout, though, is likely a reflection of greater civic interest than of the Election Day State holiday.

CONCLUSION

It is a commonly held belief that Election Day holidays result in higher voter turnout while providing local election officials with more polling places and poll workers.The data, however, do not reveal significantly higher turnout in States with Election Day State holidays. Moreover, the Election Day holiday results in some drawbacks for administrators.

There may be some benefits to the Election Day State holidays that may extend to an Election Day Federal holiday. In some Illinois jurisdictions, the county clerks offices are closed on the Election Day State holiday, which enables local election officials to focus their full attention on the election. The holiday does not necessarily help local election officials secure polling places, however, especially if the school districts decide against closing. Election Day State holidays have only minimally increased the number of State employees working as poll workers.

Maryland election officials interviewed had greater access to closed schools for polling places only because the individual counties decided to close on Election Day. The closures helped, because many school districts have security concerns about polling places in the buildings while schools are in session. Closing the schools also made it possible for several hundred students to work in the polling places on Election Day.

When comparing the nine States that have an Election Day State holiday with all the other States that do not have Election Day holidays, as well as with the United States as a whole, there appears to be no relationship between an Election Day holiday and higher voter turnout.

When comparing the nine States that have an Election Day State holiday with all the other States that do not have Election Day holidays, as well as with the United States as a whole, there appears to be no relationship between an Election Day holiday and higher voter turnout.

A NATIONAL HOLIDAY

Just as with Election Day State holidays, an Election Day Federal holiday would not require that State, county, and local governments close nor would it require school closures. Some jurisdictions might follow the Federal government and close for the day. The only certainty with establishing an Election Day Federal holiday, however, would be the cost of paying for the day off for millions of Federal employees. At this time, the turnout data regarding Election Day State holidays do not reveal higher voter turnout. The benefits usually cited to justify the holidays are mostly anecdotal.

It is inadvisable at this time to establish a legal public holiday under section 6103 of title 5, United States Code, as the date on which general elections for Federal office are held until more research can be completed.

OREGON'S VOTE-BY-MAIL

Oregon has a history of decentralized elections. Until the mid-1970s, local officials in the State's 36 counties could call for elections any time about any issue without coordinating with other electoral authorities in the State. As a result, there were frequent elections, and turnout in local contests steadily declined as voters suffered from "election fatigue."

For more than two decades, Oregon has conducted "vote-by-mail" elections. Originally, this alternative voting method was an attempt to reverse a decline in voter turnout. Now it is widely supported by the public for its convenience, and other jurisdictions and States have expressed interest in the method.

The alternative voting method began in 1981 when the Oregon Legislature approved vote-by-mail for local elections in which no candidates were on the ballot. The experiment has since evolved to include special elections, statewide elections, primaries, and Federal elections. Oregon election officials now administer all elections exclusively with vote-by-mail.

IMPLEMENTATION AND EFFECT

Election officials quickly discovered a number of differences between traditional precinct-based and vote-by-mail elections. The administration of elections becomes less complicated when the pressures involved in recruiting, training, and managing poll workers are eliminated. Similarly, without in-person voting, officials have no need to secure numerous polling places. Oregon election officials claim that voter registration lists tend to be more accurate because the frequent mailing of nonforwardable ballots provides local election officials with updated information about the actual home addresses of the voters when mail is returned as undeliverable. Furthermore, some evidence indicates that vote-by-mail elections might cost less to administer than precinct-based elections and may increase voter turnout.

Voter participation declined to the single digits for some local elections during the 1970s. While looking for an alternative way of conducting elections that would reenergize the electorate in his county, then-Multnomah County Elections Director Bill Radakovich observed a vote-by-mail election in California. That experience led him to present the potential to use the alternative voting method to the Oregon Legislature and to then-Secretary of State Norma Paulus (1977–85).

State Name:	Oregon
Chief Election Official:	Hon. Bill Bradbury,
	Secretary of State
	136 State Capitol
	Salem, OR 9731 0-0722
Number of Registered Voters:	1,994,320 (in 2006)
Alternative Voting Method:	Vote-by-Mail
Implemented:	1981

In 1981, the Oregon Legislature debated and passed a bill that allowed local jurisdictions to experiment with vote-by-mail elections in which no candidates were on the ballot. Subsequent legislation rapidly expanded the use of vote-by-mail methods that led to the practices and procedures used for vote-by-mail elections in Oregon today.

HISTORY OF VOTE-BY-MAIL

Table 2. Oregon's Vote-by-Mail Timeline of Major Events[23]

1981	The Oregon Legislature approves a test of vote-by-mail methods for local elections.
1987	Vote-by-mail is made permanent; most counties use it for local/ special elections.
June 1993	First special statewide election by mail is held—39 percent turnout.
May 1995	Second special statewide election by mail is held—44 percent turnout.
Spring/Summer 1995	The Oregon Legislature approves a proposal to expand vote-by-mail to primary and general elections. The Governor vetoes the bill. A separate bill authorizes the use of vote-by-mail for the Presidential preference primary. The Governor signs the bill into law.[24]
December 1995	Oregon becomes the first State to conduct a primary election totally by mail to nominate candidates to fill a vacancy in a Federal office—58 percent turnout.
January 1996	Oregon becomes the first State to conduct a general election totally by mail to fill a vacancy in a Federal office when it selects Senator Ron Wyden to replace Senator Bob Packwood—66 percent turnout.
March 1996	Oregon holds the country's second vote-by-mail Presidential primary. (North Dakota held the first vote-by-mail Presidential primary just weeks before Oregon's election.)—58 percent turnout.
May 1998	Primary election at the polls. Of registered voters in Oregon, 41 percent are permanent absentee voters. Overall, the State posts a record low turnout at 35 percent. Absentee ballots represent nearly two-thirds of all ballots cast; Oregon becomes the first State to have more ballots cast by mail than at the polls during a polling place election.
June 1998	Supporters of expanding vote-by-mail to primary and general elections use the initiative to put the issue on the November general election ballot.
November 1998	Oregon voters decide to expand vote-by-mail to primary and general elections by a vote of 757,204 to 334,021.
November 2000	First vote-by-mail Presidential general election is held—79.8 percent turnout.
November 2002	Vote-by-mail general election is held—69 percent turnout.
November 2004	Vote-by-mail Presidential general election is held—86.5 percent turnout.
November 2006	Vote-by-mail general election is held—70 percent turnout.

1981

> Chapter 805, Oregon Laws 1981, SECTION 1. (1) As provided in this Act and notwithstanding any contrary provision of law, a county clerk may conduct, with the supervision of the Secretary of State, an election by mail in the county or in a city or a district defined in ORS 255.012. In deciding to conduct an election by mail, the county clerk may consider requests from the governing body of the county, city or district, and shall consider whether conducting the election by mail will be economically and administratively feasible.
>
> (2) This Act applies to any election in which candidates are not listed on the ballot, other than an emergency election, held on any date other than the date of a primary or general election.
>
> SECTION 2. (1) The Secretary of State may adopt rules governing the procedures for conducting an election under this Act. The rules shall provide for uniformity in the conduct of the election throughout the electoral district in which the election is held. The Secretary of State by rule may modify the provisions of ORS chapters 254 and 255 as necessary to implement this Act.[25]

The first legislation authorizing vote-by-mail elections was very restrictive. If local election officials wanted to conduct a vote-by-mail election, the legislation required the elections division of the Secretary of State's office to first adopt an administrative authorization rule for the jurisdiction for that specific election. Still, the county clerk made the final decision about the method of voting for each local jurisdiction.

The administration of vote-by-mail elections in 1981 was notably different from the practices and procedures currently used. Vote-by-mail elections were allowed for ballot measures only (i.e., not for candidates), and the county clerk was the sole authorized official to administer vote-by-mail elections at the local level. At the time, vote-by-mail elections were conducted within a legislative framework designed for precinct-based elections. To resolve any questions about the allowable procedures for vote-by-mail elections, the Secretary of State had rulemaking authority to modify existing statutory provisions in the elections code in order to provide enough flexibility for local election officials to conduct successful vote-by-mail elections.

1983

> Chapter 199, Oregon Laws 1983, SECTION 1 (2) [This Act applies] Sections 1 and 2, chapter 805, Oregon Laws 1981, apply to any election, [in which candidates are not listed on the ballot,] other than an emergency election, held on any date other than the date of a primary or general election.[26]

The 1981 legislation was not made permanent. It expired at the end of the legislative session and needed to be reauthorized by subsequent legislation. Legislators were hesitant to permanently authorize vote-by-mail until more information was known about its effectiveness and costs. As a result, some local election officials were unwilling to commit resources for the necessary equipment and services to implement a successful vote-by-mail system because they were unsure about whether the voting method would be changed again in the near future. Furthermore, adapting operations and processes designed for precinct-based elections to those elections conducted with voteby-mail proved cumbersome.

Voter acceptance and significant increases in voter turnout, however, were encouraging. Secretary of State Norma Paulus and her successor, Barbara Roberts (1985–91), continued to encourage the use of vote-by-mail.

1987

> Chapter 357, oregon laws 1987, SECTION 4. Not later than January 1, 1989, every county in this state shall be certified by the Secretary of State as qualified to conduct an election by mail.

By the time the 1987 legislation passed, nearly all counties in Oregon were conducting some local elections with vote-by-mail. Although vote-by-mail was an optional method for use in local elections, the county clerk still made the final decision about which type of voting would be used for each election. Officials from political subdivisions of the county wanted to decide where, when, and how their elections would be conducted. This debate continued throughout the first decade of vote-by-mail.

The 1987 legislation made the option to use voteby-mail permanent for all local elections, including elections with candidates. The law, however, specifically excluded statewide primary and general elections. In the same bill, the Oregon Legislature required all county clerks to be certified to conduct vote-by-mail elections.

1993

In June, then-Secretary of State Phil Keisling (1991–99) administered the first statewide election conducted entirely with vote-by-mail in Oregon. As with the local-level introduction of vote-by-mail more than a decade before, the first statewide voteby-mail election did not include any candidates.

The initiative on the ballot, however, about urban renewal bond payments, an issue that historically had generated very low voter interest, attracted a 39 percent turnout.[27]

1995

> Oregon Laws 1995 chapter 712 SECTION 64. ORS 254.465 is amended to read:
>
> . . . A presidential preference primary election described in section 1 of this 1995 Act shall be conducted by mail in all counties, under the supervision of the Secretary of State.
>
> Except as provided in subsection (1) of this section, an election held on the date of the biennial primary or general election shall not be conducted by mail.

> A state election not described in subsections (1) or (2) of this section may be conducted by mail. The Secretary of State by rule shall direct that a state election authorized to be conducted by mail under this subsection be conducted uniformly by mail or at polling places . . .[28]

A second statewide vote-by-mail election was conducted in May 1995. The initiative on the ballot addressed district residency requirements for legislators and the use of lottery revenue for education; it garnered a turnout of 44 percent.[29]

The State conducted its first statewide election with a candidate on the ballot in 1995. Although primary and general elections were still not allowed to be conducted with vote-by-mail, Secretary of State Phil Keisling authorized the use of vote-by-mail in the primary "special election" to fill the vacancy created by the resignation of Senator Bob Packwood. Now- Senator Ron Wyden was subsequently elected to fill the vacancy in a general special election in January 1996. The election recorded a 66 percent turnout of registered voters.[30]

1996

During the regular legislative session of 1995, the Oregon Legislature attempted to require all primary and general elections to be conducted with voteby-mail. Although the House and Senate passed legislation with such a provision, Governor John Kitzhaber vetoed SB 319.[31]

During the same session, however, the Governor signed SB 928, an omnibus election law bill, which included a change in the date of the Presidential preference primary and authorized that it be conducted with vote-by-mail.[32] The State's first Presidential primary using vote-by-mail attracted 58 percent turnout.[33]

1998

The Secretary of State decided to conduct the 1998 statewide primary election as a precinct-based election. By Election Day, 41 percent of voters had requested absentee ballots, which was an increase of 300 percent over the number requesting ballots in 1992. Overall turnout for the primary election was 35 percent. Absentee ballots represented nearly two-thirds of all ballots cast, and Oregon became the first State to have more ballots cast by mail than at the polls during a precinct-based election. Turnout among individuals requesting an absentee ballot was 53 percent.[34]

The 1998 primary was a precinct-based election with an extraordinarily high rate of voting by mail. Election officials needed to pay both the costs of providing fully staffed precincts on Election Day and of processing a high number of absentee ballots. Under Oregon law, counties pay all election costs, and county election administrators estimated that an election conducted exclusively with vote-by-mail would cost about half the amount of a precinct- based election with a high rate of absentee voting.

Almost two decades after the passage of the first bill authorizing vote-by-mail, legislation to extend the provisions to all elections remained deadlocked in the Oregon Legislature. In an attempt to bypass the legislature, a group of vote-by-mail supporters qualified an initiative for the November 1998 ballot that would require that primary and general elections be conducted exclusively with vote-by-mail.

An increasing number of voters were applying for absentee ballots for the primary and general elections even though Oregon did not have a noexcuse absentee voting law. It became evident to local election officials that a growing majority of voters preferred vote-by-mail over precinct-based elections. The public was accustomed to using voteby- mail in most elections and was frustrated at not being able to do so in primary and general elections.

In November 1998, Measure 60 passed by a vote of 757,204 to 334,021 (69.4 percent "yes" to 30.6 percent "no").[35] The passage of this initiative meant that the entire 2000 Presidential election cycle would be conducted with vote-by-mail.

ESTABLISHING UNIFORM VOTE-BY-MAIL PROCEDURES

In preparation for the 2000 Presidential primary and general elections, the Secretary of State, in conjunction with the Oregon Association of County Clerks, developed the "Vote-by-Mail Procedures Manual" for election officials. County clerks had been administering statewide vote-by-mail elections since 1993 and had run a Presidential primary with vote-by-mail 4 years earlier. The goal of this first administration manual was to standardize processes and identify best practices from across the State. The manual is updated periodically, usually following biennial sessions of the Oregon Legislature.[36]

Table 3 (on the next page) highlights major events during the election cycle.

All steps in the vote-by-mail process are open for public observation. These steps include inserting blank ballots into envelopes for mailing, receiving voted ballots, verifying signatures for determining voter eligibility, inspecting ballots, and tallying votes. Before the beginning of voting, counties must file a security plan with the Secretary or State's office that describes security measures at ballot dropoff sites and for the transport of voted ballots to the central office for counting. The security plan also must include off-premises sites used during the administration of the vote-by-mail election, including the locations of vendors where the ballots are assembled and mailed.

The text of Measure 60 on the 1998 General Election ballot provided:

REQUIRES VOTE BY MAIL IN BIENNIAL PRIMARY, GENERAL ELECTIONS

RESULT OF "YES" VOTE: "Yes" vote amends existing law to require vote by mail in biennial primary, general elections.

RESULT OF "NO" VOTE: "No" vote retains current law prohibiting vote by mail in biennial primary or general elections.

SUMMARY: Current law prohibits vote by mail for biennial primary or general elections. This proposal eliminates the prohibition and requires vote by mail for biennial primary or general elections. The proposal does not affect existing law permitting the Secretary of State and county clerk to conduct other elections either at the polls or by mail.

ESTIMATE OF FINANCIAL IMPACT: County government expenditures are estimated to be reduced each Primary and General Election year by $3,021,709.[37]

Returning the Voted Ballot

Oregon election officials spent considerable time developing procedures for the return of hundreds of thousands of voted ballots—either via the mail or at dropoff sites in each county.

Election officials focused first on ensuring ballot secrecy. Most counties use a three-envelope system for each blank ballot sent out that includes a secrecy envelope, a return-mail envelope, and the original mail-out envelope, which includes the other two envelopes and the blank ballot. After the voter makes his or her selections on the ballot, he or she seals it in the secrecy envelope, which contains no information with which an individual could ascertain the voter's identity. The voter then places the secrecy envelope into the return-mail envelope on which the voter has provided identification information and a signature to prove his or her voting eligibility.

The voter then delivers the return-mail envelope to the local election office either via the U.S. Postal Service or through ballot dropoff sites. After the local election office receives the return- mail envelope, officials check the information on the envelope and validate the voter signature by signature match. After approving the signature, officials separate the ballot in the secrecy envelope from the return-mail envelope so that it cannot be associated with the voter's identification information.

A key element in the successful implementation of vote-by-mail in Oregon is the cooperation election officials receive from the U.S. Postal Service. Officials from the U.S. Postal Service help with preplanning the mass mailings of ballots. Together, the local election officials and postal officials set schedules so the volume of ballots received in any one day is not overwhelming. On Election Day, postal officials provide facility "sweeps" of mail at 8:00 p.m. and allow election officials to pick up those returned ballots, which otherwise would not be delivered until the day after the election and would not be counted, because they must be received by the election office by the close of voting on Election Day.

Table 3. Election Day Timeline[38]

60 days before Election Day	Cutoff for ballot content.
45 days before Election Day	Overseas ballots are mailed.
21 days before Election Day	Registration closes for previously unregistered voters.
14 to 18 days before Election Day	All eligible voters in election mailed a ballot. Ballot "drop sites" throughout the county may open on the day ballots are mailed.
14 days before Election Day until 8:00 pm on Election Day	Voters can return ballots to any elections office in the State in person, by mail, or via authorized ballot drop sites. Signatures on return ballot envelopes are verified against the signatures on the voter record.
7 days before Election Day	Election officials can begin opening ballot envelopes, removing and inspecting ballots, and preparing them for vote tally.
Election day	Election officials can begin tallying ballots any time during election day.
Election Day (8:00 pm)	Polls close. All ballots received by 8:00 p.m. are accepted.

Voters may also return voted ballots at ballot drop sites located throughout the counties. Most of these sites are in public buildings (e.g., city halls and libraries), where local election officials can provide supervision of the voting process. Counties are required by law to provide voting booths for voters wishing to fill out their ballots at county election offices and ballot drop sites. The election offices and drop sites remain open until 8:00 p.m. on Election Day, at which point local election officials collect all the ballots for validation and counting.

Counting the Voted Ballot

After receiving a voted ballot at the election office, the voter's eligibility must be established before the ballot can be cast and counted. Oregon's identification procedures include the comparison of the signature on the return-mail envelope with the voter's signature on file with the county clerk. Signature verifiers in election offices, who are trained periodically in handwriting analysis by the Oregon State Police, perform verification on all ballots returned. Voters whose signatures are considered "not matching" are notified that they have until the 10th day after the election to remedy a discrepancy before their ballots are invalidated.

A significant number of ballots are returned to election offices before Election Day and are ready for vote tally before the close of the polls. Starting 7 days before Election Day, officials can begin opening return-mail envelopes, removing and inspecting ballots, and preparing them for the vote tally. Election officials can begin tallying ballots any time during Election Day. As a result, the initial vote totals released on Election Day evening contain a larger portion of the results than is typical in a precinct-based election, which would not include any absentee vote totals.

ADMINISTRATIVE CHALLENGES

The move to vote-by-mail for all elections presented new difficulties for local election officials. Most of the statewide elections conducted with vote-bymail by 2000 were relatively low-turnout contests. Election officials learned that higher voter turnout elections exhibit a different trend in ballot return. During the earlier statewide elections conducted with vote-by-mail, voters tended to return their ballots early, sometimes as many as 50 percent within the first few days after receiving their blank ballots. Officials also observed a notable spike on the last 2 days of the election.

The general election ballot in 2000 included Federal, State, and local races as well as a large number of ballot measures. Election officials learned that a larger number of contests and issues equates to voters taking a longer amount of time to return their ballots. The larger number of ballots returned later in the process created a backlog for election officials. Statewide, 45 percent of the ballots returned in the 2000 general election were returned during the last 2 days of voting. The data are presented in Table 4 and Figure 4.

Table 4. Statewide Daily Ballot Returns, November 2000 Presidential Election[39]

Date	23-Oct	24-Oct	25-Oct	26-Oct	27-Oct	30-Oct	31-Oct	1-Nov	2-Nov	3-Nov	6-Nov	7-Nov	Total
No. of Ballots Returned	20,579	65,907	57,381	60,158	55,884	96,720	149,872	106,891	104,894	138,136	327,480	374,986	1,558,888
Ballots Returned as Percent of Total Ballots Cast	1.3	4.2	3.7	3.9	3.6	6.2	9.6	6.9	6.7	8.9	21.0	24.1	

The move to vote-by-mail is not without potential problems. Many opponents of vote-by-mail contend that a greater chance for fraud exists than for elections conducted in polling places. People are transient and do not always cancel their voter registrations when they move, which allows for the possibility of ballots being sent to addresses at which voters no longer live. Also, no polling place protections, such as a private voting experience or the ability to ask for help from a poll worker trained to administer elections, are in place. Proponents of the practice believe that there are ways to eliminate fraud from the process. In Oregon, all ballots are put through a signature verification process. If the signature on the absentee ballot secrecy envelope does not match the signature on file with the election official, the ballot is rejected.

The early iterations of vote-by-mail laws in Oregon required the Secretary of State's office to investigate instances of fraud, particularly in the area of voter intimidation. Concerns focused on problems ranging from forged signatures to coercion, including "ballot parties," where individuals were forced to vote a certain way, and family members influencing the votes of other family members. Then-Secretary of State Norma Paulus commissioned a number of polls on voter fraud and intimidation, but none returned any significant evidence of a problem.

During the 1990s, election officials became much more efficient in administering vote-bymail elections. Most counties converted from punchcard systems to optical scan ballots. Instead of hand-stuffing the ballots to be sent out individually, some counties contracted the work to third parties or purchased machinery to label and insert ballots for distribution. Voter registration systems were upgraded to allow for scanning registration records. Scanning facilitates electronic access to the registrar's database of voters' signatures for validation so that individual voter cards need not be used to conduct signature verifications. Finally, voter ID barcodes were added to labels to facilitate more rapid ballot accounting and signature validation.

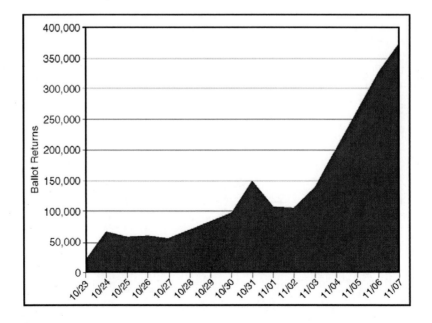

Figure 4. Cumulative Statewide Ballot Returns, November 2000 Presidential Election.

VOTERS WITH DISABILITIES

The Help America Vote Act requires that all voting systems be accessible for individuals with disabilities. This requirement results in a unique problem for administering an all vote-by-mail election. Oregon has developed a number of practices designed to meet this challenge.

For voters with vision impairments, Marion County election officials developed a ballot encased in a sleeve that contains tactile markings. While filling in the ballot, an accompanying audio tape describes the entire ballot to the voter based on the individual's appropriate ballot style. The tape also includes instructions for navigating the tactile markings.[40]

In 2004, the Secretary of State experimented with a telephone voting system for voters with disabilities, which has since been implemented in all Oregon counties. The Assistive Ballot Marking System enables voters with disabilities to mark their ballots independently using a telephone and fax machine at the county clerk's office. It was used statewide for the first time in 2006. The Secretary of State also used an HTML ballot for some voters with disabilities. Voters using this technology could download their ballots from the Secretary of State's Web site. The voter could then fill in his or her ballot on the computer, print it out, and cast it using the return ballot envelope as would any individual using vote-by-mail.[41]

VOTER TURNOUT

The Oregon Legislature initially authorized vote-bymail elections as an attempt to reverse a decrease in turnout for local elections. The belief then was that the added convenience of voting through the mail would increase turnout. Now that vote-by-mail is used for all elections in Oregon, it is reasonable to evaluate the effect of vote-by-mail on overall turnout.

A survey completed in 1996 shows that Oregon voters overwhelmingly supported vote-by-mail elections. The results also suggested, however, that voter turnout was likely to remain at levels consistent with regular precinct-based elections. In 1996, individuals choosing to cast their ballots by mail tended to resemble traditional voters rather than nonvoters; it appeared that such individuals seemed to want an easier, more convenient way to vote.

Voter turnout data from more recent elections show a different trend in participation. Turnout of registered voters has increased in each of the last two Presidential elections. During the 1996 Presidential election, which was the last one conducted as a precinct-based election, 71.3 percent of registered voters cast ballots.[42] The percentage increased to 79.8 percent during the 2000 Presidential election, which was the first election conducted exclusively with vote-by-mail.[43] The second Presidential election conducted with vote-by-mail saw another sizeable increase in percentage of turnout to 86.5 percent.[44] The 2008 election turnout figure will be useful data for evaluating the continuing effect of vote-by-mail on turnout.

Table 5. Voter Turnout by Political Party, 2000 and 2004

Year	2000[45]	2004[46]
Democrats	82.9	88.8
Republicans	85.6	89.7
Nonaffilliated	67.4	78.9
other	60.7	76.1
Total	79.8	86.5

Some debate by party officials and political scientists throughout the 25 years Oregon has used vote-by-mail has centered on whether a political party might gain an advantage with voteby-mail elections as compared with traditional precinct-based voting. It appears that the increases in turnout seen in the past three Presidential elections, though, were bipartisan. The turnout in the 2000 Presidential election was the highest the State had seen since 1964, and each major party showed similar levels of increase. Turnout among nonaffiliated and third-party voters increased the most, by nearly 14 and 16 percent, respectively.

LEGAL CHALLENGES

The most significant legal dispute over Oregon's vote-by-mail elections was a lawsuit in Federal court challenging the State's authority to expand voting in Federal elections beyond Election Day. The Voting Integrity Project's position was that the U.S. Constitution provides that the first Tuesday after the first Monday in November is established "...as the exclusive day throughout the United States for balloting for United States Representatives, United States Senators, and Presidential Electors." Thus the argument was that the election was taking place before Election Day.

In upholding the District Court's ruling against the plaintiffs, the 9th Circuit found that "the Supreme Court has provided the device for reconciling the federal election day statute and the federal absentee voting statute: a definition of 'election' that treats election day as the 'consummation' of the process rather than any day during which voting takes place. Given that definition, and the force of the absentee voting statute, Oregon is in compliance with the federal election day statute. Although voting takes place, perhaps most voting, prior to election day, the election is not 'consummated' before election day because voting still takes place on that day."[47]

ACADEMIC STUDIES

The special election in 1996 to fill the vacancy in one of Oregon's seats in the U.S. Senate was one of the first statewide vote-by-mail elections to include candidates. Shortly after the election, three academic studies were released about various aspects of the vote-by-mail alternative voting method. The studies covered a range of topics, including the attitudes about vote-by-mail, the demographics of individuals using vote-by-mail as compared with precinct-based voters, the method of ballot return, and the presence or absence of fraud and intimidation in vote-by-mail elections.

Vote-by-mail is an alternative voting method that has attracted much national attention. An overwhelming majority (76.5 percent) of the 1,225 respondents to South well's survey favored vote-bymail elections over polling place elections.

Priscilla L. Southwell of the University of Oregon completed a survey about the demographics of vote-by-mail voters. According to Southwell's data, vote-by-mail voters tend to resemble traditional voters rather than nonvoters, meaning that voteby-mail would be unlikely to increase the turnout of new voters. It appears that those using vote-by-mail are traditional voters who want an easier, more convenient way to vote.

Vote-by-mail is an alternative voting method that has attracted much national attention. An overwhelming majority (76.5 percent) of the 1,225 respondents to Southwell's survey favored vote-by-mail elections over polling place elections. Her research, however, also suggests that the consequences of vote-by-mail are far less dramatic—with lower increases in voter turnout and fewer party advantages—than others had suggested.[48]

Michael W. Traugott of the University of Michigan and Robert G. Mason of Oregon State University focused their study on election administration. Eighty-five percent of voters reported mailing in their ballots, and 15 percent indicated they dropped off their ballots. Traugott and Mason noted that women were more likely to mail their ballots than were men. Voters cited four main reasons for dropping off their ballots: (1) it was more convenient (42 percent); (2) they had no time to mail the ballot (23 percent); (3) it saves postage (16 percent); (4) it ensures the ballot arrives safely (8 percent).[49]

David Magelby of Brigham Young University researched the return of voted ballots. Specifically, his research focused on the timeliness of the return of voted ballots. He identified three periods during the ballot return window: January 10–17, January 18–23, and January 24–30. Magelby asked three questions: (1) Does vote-by-mail create an advantage or disadvantage for a particular candidate or party? (2) Is one political party more able to mobilize voters early in the process? (3) How many days should be given to voters to return their mail ballots?

The most important conclusion to be drawn from Magelby's data is that the results within each time period do not significantly differ from the final result. The final election result would have remained the same even if voting had ended on January 17 or January 23. With this information, it appears that neither party had an advantage during any part of the extended campaign process. Supporters of both candidates behaved similarly in all three time periods, and the results favored the eventual winner at the end of all three time periods. Administrators might be able to use this initial assessment to justify shortening the voting period by several days without altering the outcome of an election in order to save on election administration expenses.[50]

CONCLUSION

It is possible that vote-by-mail increases turnout; however, other benefits to vote-by-mail are unassociated with voter turnout. For example, local election officials do not need to spend any time securing traditional polling places. They do not need to recruit, train, and retain poll workers from election to election. Without these tasks, election officials can direct their focus toward ballot production, distribution, and counting. Specifically, some administrators cite the top benefit as improved oversight of the election, because most of the process occurs within the elections office or a vote processing facility instead of in hundreds of precincts staffed by poll workers.

The most important conclusion to be drawn from Magelby's data is that the results within each time period do not significantly differ from the final result.

Former Multnomah County Election Director Vicki Ervin believes that vote-by-mail has benefited her county. Vote-by-mail removes some of the traditional barriers to voting, such as inaccessible polling places and arranging transportation to and from polling places. She notes that voters have a more thorough understanding of the issues because the ballot is provided early enough in the process for the voter to study it along with any explanatory materials provided.

Vote-by-mail is widely supported by both the public in Oregon and election administrators across the State. It may increase participation for both low- and high-turnout contests, and it is likely to expand in the future election cycles.

COLORADO VOTE CENTERS

Vote centers are an alternative method of voting that provides additional convenience to voters on Election Day. Instead of using traditional neighborhood precincts, voters choose to vote in any one of the larger, strategically located polling sites throughout the county on Election Day.

More than 20 counties in Colorado have used the vote center model in at least one election. This section examines the implementation of vote centers in two counties: Larimer and Denver. In 2003, Larimer County effectively established vote centers and has used them in subsequent elections. Denver County's first experience with them in 2006, however, was less successful. Even so, in 2008 Denver County plans to use "super precincts," which differ from vote centers because voters are assigned to them and are not able to choose for themselves the most convenient location at which to vote. In essence, they are the aggregation of many precincts into one large polling place.

Although only a small number of elections have been administered with vote centers, preliminary research points to potential increases in turnout. The concept is so new that it will take time for policymakers to determine where it is best used and where it is least desirable. More research is necessary to determine the effect of vote centers, but the new concept seems to have more positive than negative consequences.

IMPLEMENTATION AND EFFECT

According to data collected during the 2004 and 2006 Federal elections, finding a polling place is one of the biggest difficulties faced by a voter on Election Day.[51] Small precincts are sometimes located in places with which some voters are unfamiliar. Alternatively, vote centers are located in high-profile, major-traffic areas rather than in neighborhood schools or churches. Each voter decides for himself or herself where it would be most convenient to vote that day. This new method of voting could reduce the number of provisional ballots needed each election, because any registered voter can choose to vote in any vote center.

State Name:	Colorado
Alternative Voting Method:	Vote centers
Larimer county chief Election official:	Scott Doyle
Active Registered Voters:	154,540 (in 2006)
Precincts	153
Vote centers	30
implemented:	2003
Denver county chief Election official:	Wayne Vaden
Active Registered Voters:	287,839 (in 2006)
Precincts	423
Vote centers	55
implemented:	2006

The 2000 Presidential election was a turning point for election administration. Election officials across the country began assessing their systems and planning for the future. In Larimer County, ideas were already being developed for a voting experiment that would enable citizens to vote at any one of many polling sites located in high-profile, major-traffic areas. It was in this context that a new alternative to traditional voting methods emerged— the alternative was called a "vote center."

Vote centers are easier for local election officials to administer than are a multitude of smaller polling places. First, there are fewer Americans with Disabilities Act (ADA)-compliant polling locations to find and manage. Fewer polling locations equates to fewer administrative hurdles for local election officials. Administrators can recruit the most efficient poll workers to serve on Election Day when they do not need to staff hundreds of small, individual precincts. Second, fewer provisional ballots need to be issued, because a registered individual cannot vote in the "wrong" polling place, which increases the likelihood that ballots will be counted correctly as individuals vote with regular ballots. Finally, the larger polling locations also benefit from economies of scale, leading to more adequate parking logistics and a more effective deployment of resources.

The success or failure of the vote center concept begins with the planning and preparation before Election Day. Vote centers require significantly more training—and more specialized training—for staff and poll workers. For example, Larimer County poll workers are required to complete 8 hours of training before working in a vote center. Poll workers are also trained for the specific job function they will fulfill on Election Day.

To closely estimate the amount of supplies and/or number of voting machines for each vote center, administrators must predict where voters will vote. No concrete formula is available to help an administrator determine the best allocation of electronic poll books, voting machines, paper ballots, and poll workers throughout his or her county. In Larimer County, the practice has been to overestimate what is needed and to have extra resources ready to be delivered to vote centers as necessary throughout Election Day.

If vote centers are to be successful, the county must use an electronic poll book, which tracks real-time voter information and benefits both administrators and candidates. Administrators see where more resources might be necessary because of higher turnout in one vote center over another. The political parties and candidates receive electronically generated lists created throughout the day, enabling them to alter their getout-the-vote efforts.

COLORADO VOTING OPTIONS

Permanent Mail-in Balloting
Thirty days before Election Day, ballots are mailed to voters who have requested them. The voted ballots must be returned to the elections office before the close of the polls on Election Day.

Early Voting
Early voting in Colorado begins two weeks before Election Day; early voting sites are open from 8:00 a.m. to 5:00 p.m., weekdays.

Election Day
Larimer County uses 30 vote centers instead of 153 precincts. The five early voting sites convert to vote centers on Election Day, when polls are open from 7:00 a.m. to 7:00 p.m.

LEGISLATIVE HISTORY

After Larimer County successfully completed its first vote center election in 2003, election officials approached the Colorado Legislature about permitting the use of the vote center model in general election years. At the time, Colorado law did not allow for the combining of precincts for general elections. The Colorado Legislature passed Senate bill 04-153, which permitted the use of vote centers in general elections, but only if the State's other voting procedures were not affected.

There are other legal considerations for election officials using vote centers in Colorado. The vote centers must be equipped with secure electronic connections for the poll book. The county clerk is required to consult with all of the major and minor parties during site selection and must have one vote center for every 10,000 voters.[52]

LARIMER COUNTY LAUNCHES VOTE CENTERS

Larimer County Clerk and Recorder Scott Doyle and his staff began planning for the use of vote centers in early 2003, and the model was used for the first time in the November 2003 election. Colorado law at that time already allowed precincts to be combined in off-year elections.

Costs

One of the first issues to address was the cost of implementing vote centers and figuring out how to cover the expense within the existing 2003 budget. Larimer County elections staff developed a business plan that identified all financial components of a vote center election and included a contingency amount of roughly 5 percent to allow for unforeseen problems. Vote centers require larger polling locations than do traditional precincts; however, the economies of scale created by using the vote center model mitigate some of the costs of administering an election, and local officials need fewer poll workers, sites, and machines.

One new expense stemming from the vote center model is the electronic poll book. In 2003, Larimer County made an additional expenditure of $165,000; however, the extra expense for the electronic poll book technology is a one-time cost.

Educating the Public

Early in the process, local officials contracted with an outside public relations expert to address the voter education challenges of the project. Because vote centers represented a major change to the traditional voting process, it was deemed necessary by election officials to develop a comprehensive plan for systematically informing voters of, and preparing them for, the new system of voting on Election Day.

The elections office conducted several mailings. The first mailer, which went to all county voters in May 2003, contained a letter from the county clerk addressing the change and explaining what it would mean to voters. As an added convenience, an absentee ballot request form was included for voters wishing to avoid the new system. A second mailer sent to all voters in September 2003—timed to encourage early voting—included a signature card that voters were encouraged to bring to the vote center to expedite the voting process.

A key element of the public relations campaign was to direct all voters to the county clerk's elections Web page.[53] Other traditional methods, however, were also used. With the help of the outside public relations expert, the elections office compiled a contact list of media organizations. The county clerk wrote editorials for local newspapers. The elections office purchased advertising in affordable media and distributed fact sheets and fliers depicting the vote center experience to the public. The clerk's office developed a newsletter in house and sent it out electronically each quarter to those who expressed interested. This newsletter continues to provide an ongoing outlet for important election dates and events.

KEY ELEMENTS IN LARIMER COUNTY VOTE CENTERS

- Each vote center is designed to accommodate more voters than are reasonably expected. For example, if the highest expected usage is 3,500, the center is designed to handle 5,000.
- The electronic poll book is designed to process a voter every 30 seconds.
- Each center is equipped with enough electronic poll books to serve the number of voters expected. Large turnout sites begin the day with 8 to 10 poll books.
- Vote centers allow for the use of paper ballots or electronic voting.
- The ballot station is set up to handle a paper or electronic voter every 10 seconds.
- Based on estimated turnout volume and the type of voting equipment used, 2 to 20 electronic voting machines and 5 to 40 voting booths are located at each vote center.

Technology and Logistics

Each vote center is unique and requires a different setup to operate efficiently. In heavily populated areas, vote centers are configured to process up to 5,000 voters on Election Day. The successful use of vote centers requires choosing an adequately large site, having appropriate technology and ballots in place, and ensuring judges are adequately trained. Less populated areas of the county require smaller vote centers.

Most Larimer County vote centers are 1,500 to 2,500 square feet, with some as large as 3,000 square feet. Parking for at least 80 cars is suggested, and each vote center must comply with the ADA according to the U.S. Department of Justice's guide for polling places.[54]

Larimer County purchased and installed T-1 lines (cables capable of quickly transferring electronic data), routers, and switches in vote center locations. Officials tested all electronics before Election Day to ensure the system functioned properly.

The computers used to check voters in at vote centers came from various county departments that had upgraded their computer systems. These surplus computers had been scheduled for replacement by other departments, so no cost was associated with their procurement. Today, computers are cycled out as "new" retired units become available from other departments of the local government.

Larimer County already had six servers that could handle the load of data on Election Day. The electronic poll book developed in house included a reduced amount of voter registration data to allow fast operation and easy training for judges. The entire system runs parallel to the Internet and allows for secure sockets layer, which is the same security used in online banking worldwide. With this real-time technology, a voter checks in at a vote center and receives instant credit for voting on the master poll book.

The electronic poll book has many benefits. First, it enables election staff to monitor vote center operations from the elections office as the day progresses to determine the ballot supply needs at the vote centers. This enhanced management tool is extremely useful for keeping voters moving through the process. Also, candidate and party poll watching is simplified with electronic poll book technology. As the day progresses, the county clerk develops an electronic list of who has voted. The elections office supplies the list to any campaign or party requesting the information, which enables get-out-the-vote campaign phone workers to use it immediately.

Before the use of vote centers, poll workers in Larimer County picked up precinct equipment and supplies early on Election Day morning and returned them after the polls closed. With vote centers, much of the workload occurs the day before and the day after Election Day. The day before an election, a moving company delivers equipment and supplies to vote centers. A team of technology experts arrives just after the moving company and arranges the center as specified in a predesigned site plan. The team wires and tests all technology at that time to ensure proper operation.

Larimer County attempted to identify all issues that might arise on Election Day by calculating how long it takes to serve one voter, multiplying that time by the number of voters expected, and then factoring in "what if" scenarios. It is difficult to identify all that might go wrong during an election, but Larimer County's vote center model contains contingency measures that can be implemented if needed. In addition, one key to success is the rigorous testing and retesting of all systems.

VOTE CENTER STAFFING

Each vote center is staffed with a supervisor, troubleshooter, and judges.

- The **supervisor** is a specially trained staff member of the clerk's office or an election judge who has gained experience in a supervisory capacity during the previous 2 weeks of early voting. The supervisor is responsible for all Election Day activities at his or her assigned vote center. Supervisors assist troubleshooters and judges and are responsible for overseeing all processes at the vote center. The supervisor is equipped with a cell phone so that he or she can establish contact quickly with the clerk, election director, or main election office when needed.
- In many cases, a **troubleshooter** is a staff member from the clerk's office. Troubleshooters are responsible for traffic flow through the vote center and for identifying technology issues that arise. The troubleshooter reports directly to the vote center supervisor.
- **Election judges** are recruited and chosen for vote centers in several ways. Political parties supply most of the judges in Larimer County, and the clerk's office staff and other county employees are recruited to assist as needed. A "student judge" program has been developed using students from area high schools.

A well-balanced mix of judges is necessary. Although a direct need exists for qualified judges who can handle technology issues, there are many other activities to be accomplished within a vote center. Judges less familiar with technology are put to work greeting voters, handing out ballots, and seeing voters out after they complete voting.

Judges are trained for the specific job function they will be expected to accomplish on Election Day. Currently, the Larimer County election staff trains judges in house, but election officials have considered using an outside trainer for future election cycles. General training lasts 3 hours in the morning, and the afternoon is spent training to perform the specific job function the staffer will handle on Election Day.

THE PHYSICAL LAYOUT OF A VOTE CENTER

Each vote center consists of multiple "stations" (see Figure 5).Greeters welcome voters, electronic poll book judges check them in, ballot judges provide the voter with the proper ballot, escorts help voters to the voting booth or digital recording electronic (DRE) voting machine, ballot deposit judges oversee the scanning and deposit of ballots, and judges stationed at the provisional ballot table help voters with provisional ballots.

Greeter

Upon arrival, a greeter welcomes the voter, asks if the person brought the personal signature card that was mailed the previous week, and checks the voter's identification. The voter is asked to fill out a signature card (if he/she did not bring the preprinted form) and is then routed to the next station. Each vote center is designed so that lines move at a rate of 100 feet every 30 minutes.

Computer Station

The next station is the electronic poll book where the voter shows the proper identification and signature card. Vote centers have multiple electronic poll book stations, and each is designed to process a voter in 30 seconds or less. (Many voters finish their experience at this station within as little as 15 to 20 seconds.) The voter is given credit for voting on the master poll book and routed to the next station.

Provisional Ballot Table

If a voter experiences a problem (e.g., not listed in the poll book or not having appropriate ID), the person is routed to the provisional ballot table. At the provisional ballot table, the voter provides the required information, signs an affidavit, receives an appropriate ballot, and is routed to the voting booth/ DRE to vote the ballot.

Ballot Station

Voters at the ballot station are provided with the appropriate ballot style.

Voting Booth

From the ballot station, the voter is directed to a voting booth/DRE and left alone to vote.

Exit

After voting is complete, the voter deposits the paper ballot or DRE voter access card with the judge located near the exit door.

IMPACT OF LARIMER COUNTY VOTE CENTERS

According to Larimer County Clerk Scott Doyle, the use of vote centers has significantly improved access to voting. Instead of many small precinct- based polling locations, a fewer number of large vote center facilities are used, and voters simply choose the one that is most convenient for them. In a culture where home, work, and recreation facilities may be distributed all across a metropolitan area and where extensive commuting is the norm, it makes sense to do what retailers have done for decades—provide multiple convenient locations for mobile Americans. Administratively, vote centers are easier to manage, improve overall efficiency, and reduce Election Day issues for election officials if they are properly planned and implemented.

Voter Turnout

Total voter turnout has increased following the introduction of vote centers, as demonstrated in Table 6. Although the implementation of vote centers coupled with early voting, absentee voting, and the decrease in provisional voting for individuals attempting to vote out of precinct on Election Day contributed to higher turnout, voting on the actual Federal Election Day did decrease from 2000 to 2004 after the implementation of vote centers. EAC researchers will need to follow the vote center concept over several more election cycles to evaluate the effectiveness of the alternative voting method to increase voter turnout.

Poll Workers

The use of vote centers decreased the number of Election Day judges needed by 50 percent compared with the number needed when the county used the precinct-based model of voting. From a practical perspective, the use of vote centers means election administrators have fewer facilities to manage and fewer poll workers to recruit, train, retain, and pay.

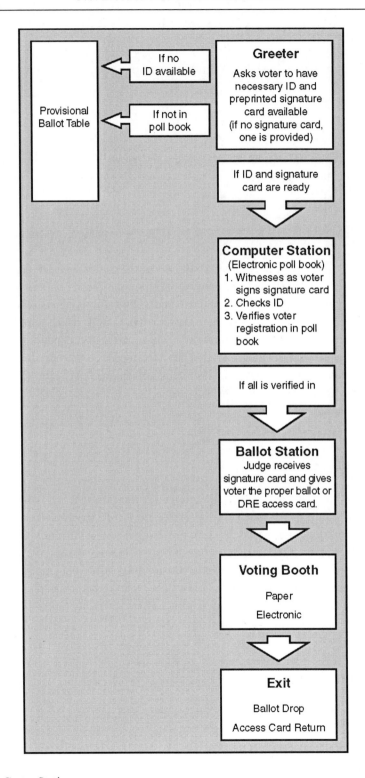

Figure 5. Vote Center Stations.

Table 6. Larimer County Election Year Totals

Election	Year	Total Registered	Early Voted					Total Early Voted	Vote Center or Precinct Voting	Total Voted	%
			Early Voting	Absentee							
		Poll Book		Mail	Walkout	Total Absentee					Total Voted / Reg
General	2004	199,129	45,718	46,941	174	47,115	92,933	52,481	147,112	78.88
General	2002	188,168	8,325	35,651	1,584	37,235	45,560	48,919	95,276	50.63
General	2000	191,124	13,769	40,355	7,278	47,633	61,402	57,582	119,201	62.37
General	1998	166,700	10,969	13,877	5,524	19,401	30,370	56,484	86,875	52.11

Denver's Vote Center Experience

Colorado law allows any county to the vote center model, and 20 have done so with few problems.[55] Douglas County encountered issues the vote center model for the first time in the November 2006 general election, but those issues were likely an underestimation of resources needed and the way those resources were allocated.

The 2006 primary and midterm elections in Denver did not go smoothly. An investigative review panel formed by the Mayor of Denver, John Hickenlooper, reported the following issues with Denver's vote center model:[56]

Check-in

Electronic poll books did not work efficiently, which made it difficult to move voters to the next step expeditiously.

Voting Equipment

Lines formed because not enough electronic voting machines were available to handle the volume of voters.

Ballots

A shortage of provisional (paper) ballots contributed to the long lines.

Educating the Public

Denver may have benefited from hiring an outside consultant to develop a comprehensive communication plan for advertising and explaining vote centers. Larimer County spent considerable time and resources on this step during its implementation of the alternative voting method. The Larimer County elections officials explained to voters how a vote center works and that alternative voting options such as absentee and early voting were available.

Vote center Design and Setup

Denver complied with the law governing the minimum number of vote centers—at least one per 10,000 voters. It is not clear is how Denver estimated voter turnout and whether Denver's contingency measures addressed larger than normal turnout.

Even if the poll book technology had worked well in Denver, trouble may still have occurred at voting machines. Denver estimated that each voter would need to minutes to access and vote the ballot, but the 2006 ballot was Colorado's longest ballot in a century—resulting in slower voting and longer lines.

Technology

It was reported that the electronic poll book had problems during the absentee voting period; however, the poll book was not tested before Election Day.[57] As was demonstrated in Larimer County, routine testing and monitoring of equipment, software, and network performance is crucial to the success of the vote center model.

Contingency Measures

Denver had contingency measures in place, but it is not clear whether they were activated within a reasonable window of time. An ideal response would be the deployment of staff to any given location within minutes. Denver had no manual backup in place to guide voters through the voting process.

ACADEMIC STUDY

Professor Robert M. Stein of Rice University studied vote center use in Larimer County to test the hypothesis that Election Day vote centers positively influence turnout among nonhabitual voters.[58]

Stein suggests that the cost of voting is largely tied to the time and inconvenience associated with the act of voting. Previous electoral reforms, such as early voting and absentee voting, may not have effectively addressed this aspect of the cost of voting. As such, these reforms may have failed to remedy the inconvenience of voting and may have benefited only those who would have voted anyway. Stein's study examines the convenience afforded by vote centers and the effect on turnout.

Stein's study indicates that a change in polling locations has two effects:

1. Transportation effect resulting from change in distance.
2. Disruption effect resulting from information required to locate a voting site.

Together, these findings may suggest that the convenience and accessibility of a voter's Election Day voting location is a significant factor in whether or not he or she will vote. Stein reports that the reported popularity of early voting suggests that many voters prefer the convenience afforded by accessible voting locations, short lines, and assistance in using new, unfamiliar voting technologies. Therefore, it is reasonable to assume that voter turnout may increase if more voter convenience is introduced into Election Day balloting through vote centers.

Although Stein's research includes data from only a few elections administered with vote centers, the aggregate-level findings suggest that Election Day vote centers may account for an increase in overall turnout in Larimer County.

CONCLUSION

Vote centers have had mixed success in Colorado. Larimer County has used the alternative voting method successfully, but Denver has decided not to use it in 2008. When local election officials administer vote centers correctly, it appears that vote centers have a positive effect on overall turnout. Although overall turnout increased, actual voting on Election Day decreased from 2000 to 2004 in Larimer County. Moreover, it is still not known if the increase in overall turnout seen so far is sustainable.

The use of vote centers is popular when everything works efficiently, and it is advisable to explore further the alternative voting method for its effectiveness and use in future elections and for its expansion to other jurisdictions.

WEEKEND VOTING

Federal law requires that elections for Federal office occur on the first Tuesday after the first Monday in November. Yet, the traditional Tuesday Election Day is predicated on the needs of an agrarian society and may not still be the most optimal day on which Americans should vote. Weekend voting has been used as an alternative voting method with the belief that it might provide more convenience to voters and increase voter turnout.

Weekend voting for Federal elections is not without potential drawbacks. For example, it may make it more difficult for some local election officials to recruit sufficient poll workers and to find suitable polling places. Voting on a weekend might cost more because most States require overtime pay for employees on the weekends. Although weekend voting may result in higher turnout for some State and local elections, the added benefits of weekend voting when compared with Tuesday Election Day for Federal elections are less clear.

EAC researchers chose Louisiana, Texas, and Delaware to highlight for this case study. In each of these States, jurisdictions either currently conduct or have conducted some form of weekend voting. Federal elections cannot be conducted exclusively on weekends under current law. Therefore, it is impossible for researchers to gather good comparative data about the effect of weekend voting on Federal elections. It is still possible, however, to explore the potential benefits and drawbacks of a possible move to weekend voting by looking at the election administration of weekend voting for State and local elections.

It should also be noted that jurisdictions have different conceptions of weekend voting. The studies of Louisiana and Delaware reflect only a Saturday Election Day. The most recently introduced related legislation in the Senate, the Weekend Voting Act, as well as almost all Federal legislation to move Election Day to the weekend, would establish a new Federal Election Day as the "first Saturday and Sunday after the first Friday in November."[59] EAC considers "weekend voting" to be a 2-day Election Day that takes place on both Saturday and Sunday.

Jurisdiction Name:	East Feliciana Parish, Louisiana
Chief Election official:	Hon. Debbie D. Hudnall East Feliciana Parish Clerk of Court P.O. Drawer 599 Clinton, LA 70722
Number of Registered Voters:	13,371
Alternative Voting Method:	Weekend Voting
Implemented:	1959

Jurisdiction Name:	Harris county, TX
Chief Election official:	Beverly Kaufman, County Clerk 1001 Preston Avenue Houston, TX 77251
Number of Registered Voters:	1,804,641
Alternative Voting Method:	Weekend Voting
Implemented:	1975

Jurisdiction Name:	New castle county, Delaware
Chief Election official:	Elaine Manlove, Director of Elections 820 N. French Street New castle, DE 19801
Number of Registered Voters:	358,705
Alternative Voting Method:	Weekend Voting
Implemented:	1978

IMPLEMENTATION AND EFFECT

The studies provide useful data about turnout in local and State elections on Saturdays. In Louisiana, all elections except Federal contests occur on Saturdays. In the past, Delaware conducted its primaries on a Saturday. The Texas study, however, may be the most instructive when evaluating the efficacy of moving Federal Election Day from Tuesday to weekend voting. The weekend voting in the Texas study represents the portion of the 12-day early voting period that occurs on Saturdays and Sundays. Still, an evaluation of voting patterns during the entire Texas early voting period reveals no rise in voting on Saturdays and Sundays when put in context with the other days during the early voting period. It is impossible to determine from the data whether turnout would have been the same if voting had taken place on Saturday and Sunday exclusively.

Some differences between Tuesday Election Day and weekend voting that can be examined are the administrative costs and challenges. A rough cost comparison between Tuesday Election Day costs and weekend Election Day costs can be made by local election officials of any additional costs that might be incurred if Federal elections were moved to the weekend. The studies indicate that some additional costs are incurred related to holding Saturday Election Days versus Tuesday Election Days. Saturday elections are likely to cost more per day because of higher weekend pay for facility maintenance and security personnel, overtime pay for election staff, and the increased cost to rent polling places. The cost could increase substantially if the 1-day Tuesday Election Day is changed to 2 days of weekend voting. In addition, some costs associated with a 2-day election are not incurred during a 1-day election, such as overnight ballot and polling place security.

Voter convenience is usually the main argument in favor of moving Federal Election Day to weekend voting. For example, because most of the workforce works during the regular business week, weekend voting could make it easier and, presumably, more likely for voters to go to the polls. Similarly, without voting on a traditional workday, there might be less of morning and evening rush voting periods that result in long lines. Although local election officials interviewed thought that weekend voting might reduce wait time at the polls, there were no data with which to evaluate the hypothesis.

Weekends are not necessarily more convenient than Tuesday Election Days for all voters. Both Saturday and Sunday are religious days for groups of voters. Any organized push to weekend voting is likely to be met with strong opposition from Jewish and Christian groups.

Most arguments against the implementation of weekend voting stem from the added administrative challenges for local election officials. Ballot integrity and polling place security measures must be rewritten to account for the new 2-day Election Day. Keeping ballots and polling places secure overnight is not an issue that most local election officials deal with during Tuesday Election Day voting if they do not use early voting. After devising secure systems, local election officials would likely have to pay for the additional security costs without Federal or State help.

Weekends are not necessarily more convenient than Tuesday Election Days for all voters. Both Saturday and Sunday are religious days for groups of voters. Any organized push to weekend voting is likely to be met with strong opposition from Jewish and Christian groups. Delaware legislators and election officials witnessed this backlash from the Jewish community regarding Saturday primary elections. The Delaware Legislature eventually decided to move the primaries back to Tuesdays.

Even though a voter may not be working if Election Day is conducted during the weekend, it is unclear whether that scenario means that voting becomes a priority for the individual. Weekends are often spent on leisure time, and no evidence exists to indicate that voting would become a priority during weekend voting if it is not already a priority to an individual on traditional Tuesday Election Days. Such a move to weekend voting may instead lead to an increase in demand for absentee ballots, but only 31 States currently offer no-excuse absentee voting.[60]

Local election officials interviewed reported mixed experiences about locating enough polling places for weekend voting. Some reported no added difficulty in finding enough polling places. Others found it difficult to secure polling places on weekends because facilities and maintenance staff are required to be on site in public buildings used as polling places, and local elections officials do not control those staff members. Churches and synagogues previously used for voting would likely no longer be available. Some community centers use their facilities more on the weekends than they do during the week, which may result in their unavailability to serve as polling places for weekend voting.

No information supports the conclusion that more poll workers are available for weekend voting than for Tuesday Election Day. Election officials noted that they would recruit poll workers from a different pool for weekend voting. For example, teachers would be available to work on weekends, but not on Tuesdays, unless the jurisdiction observes an Election Day holiday.

WEEKEND VOTING IN LOUISIANA

Saturday Election Day was introduced in Louisiana in 1959 for gubernatorial primaries and extended to gubernatorial general elections in 1975. In both cases, the move away from a Tuesday Election Day to a Saturday Election Day was meant to benefit the voters in the workforce.

Louisiana election officials believe that conducting non-Federal elections on Saturday is a benefit, because it makes voting more convenient for the individual voter. It may also be a benefit because voters feel less rushed in the polling place, being that they have fewer concerns about work schedules on the weekends. A local election official interviewed believes that Saturday voting results in fewer poll worker errors, because voting is spread out during the day without the "crunch times" experienced on Tuesday Election Days before work, during the lunch hour, and after work.

Administrative Challenges

Local election officials have been recruiting poll workers for Saturday Election Days for decades. Most elections in Louisiana take place on Saturdays; only Federal elections are conducted on a Tuesday Election Day. Some parish clerks explained that it makes little difference to them whether they are conducting elections on Tuesdays or Saturdays because the same number of poll workers is required. In fact, some parish clerks indicated that they find it slightly more difficult to recruit individuals to work as poll workers for Tuesday Election Days than for Saturday Election Days.

2006 ELECTIONS CALENDAR

Saturday, January 21: propositions only.
Saturday, April 1: municipal primary.
Saturday, April 29: municipal general.
Saturday, July 15: propositions only.
Saturday, September 30: open primary.
Tuesday, November 7: open general! congressional.
Saturday, December 9: congressional runoffs.

> *Note: La. Rev. Stat. Ann. § R.S. 18:402(G) (2008) prohibits elections from being conducted on certain Jewish holidays.*

Furthermore, Louisiana law requires that all public buildings be available to host a polling place on Election Day without any cost to the parish.[61] Local election officials report that this law makes it easier for them to secure polling place facilities than it is for their counterparts in other States that do not have such a law. Most polling places are in public buildings, such as schools, fire stations, and town halls, and the officials make only limited use of private buildings, including churches. Therefore, Saturday Election Day does not significantly affect the local election officials' ability to find sufficient space for polling places.

Voter Turnout

Voter turnout depends on the type of election being conducted. Federal elections result in higher turnout than do State and local elections. In 2000 and 2004, statewide turnout for the Presidential elections on Tuesdays was 63.5 percent and 66.9 percent, respectively.[62] The statewide gubernatorial elections of 1999, 2003, and 2007- all conducted on Saturdays- showed wide variations in turnout from between 26.4 and 50.9 percent.[63] Local election officials interviewed believe that there would be no difference in turnout if a Federal election were conducted on a Saturday as opposed to a Tuesday. Similarly, they did not believe that there would be a difference in turnout for a gubernatorial election if it were to be conducted on a Tuesday instead of a Saturday. They believed that turnout depends on the measures and/or candidates on the ballot.

WEEKEND VOTING IN HARRIS COUNTY, TEXAS

Weekend voting in Texas is used for both Federal and non-Federal elections. A few non-Federal elections take place on the second Saturday in May. That day is set aside for general elections for cities and schools. Although Federal elections, by law, occur on Tuesdays, the Texas law that created early voting in 1987 led to a *de facto* introduction of weekend voting for Federal elections. The 12 days of early voting in Texas must include one weekend.

Administrative Challenges

According to local election officials, early voting does affect their ability to a recruit a sufficient number of poll workers. To conduct early voting for 12 days, Harris County local election officials need to hire poll workers as temporary employees at higher rates than they pay Election Day poll workers. Should Texas move away from a process that includes both a period of early voting and a Tuesday Election Day to a system of just weekend voting, however, it is unclear if the higher pay would be necessary.

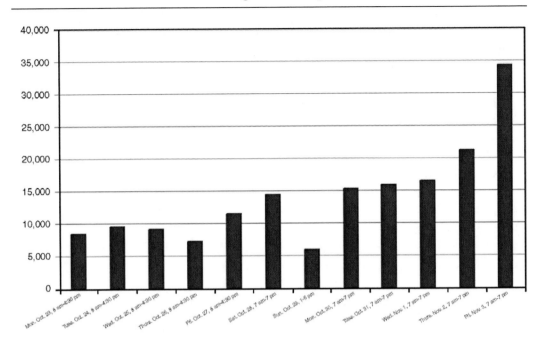

Figure 6. Daily Voter Turnout in Harris County, Texas, November 2006.

> Harris county conducts 12 days of early voting, which spans two weekends. Because the hours of operation at early voting locations fluctuate during the early voting period, it is difficult to make comparisons between weekday and weekend voting turnout.
> First Saturday in period: 1:00 p.m.–6:00 p.m.
> First Sunday in period: 1:00 p.m.–6:00 p.m.
> Monday through Friday: 8:00 a.m.–4:30 p.m.
> Second Saturday in period: 7:00 a.m.–7:00 p.m.
> Second Sunday in period: 1:00 p.m.–6:00 p.m.

It costs local election officials more to rent polling places for Saturday voting because State law allows the owner of a polling place to charge an additional fee for overtime and administrative overhead on top of the base rate. The average extra cost for a polling place on a Saturday is $250 according to the local election officials interviewed. Polling place availability, though, is not a problem for the weekend days of early voting. City and county buildings, libraries, and community centers are secured for the entire early voting period.

Voter Turnout

Harris County election officials believe that voter turnout depends on the type of election and on the measures and candidates on the ballot rather than on the day on which the election is held.

- Tuesday, November 7, 2006, general election turnout: 31.59 percent.

- Tuesday, November 8, 2005, municipal election turnout: 17.96 percent.
- Tuesday, November 2, 2004, Presidential election turnout: 58.03 percent.
- Saturday, May 15, 2004, city of Houston special bond election turnout: 8.81 percent.

Harris County election officials believe that voter turnout depends on the type of election and on the measures and candidates on the ballot rather than on the day on which the election is held.

Although turnout during the November 2006 general election spiked slightly on Saturday, October 28 (see Figure 6), it is the general expectation that more people will vote each day of early voting as Election Day approaches. The dip in voting on Sunday, October 29, could be attributed to the relatively fewer number of hours during which the early voting sites are open compared with the number of hours on the other days of early voting.

WEEKEND VOTING IN NEW CASTLE COUNTY, DELAWARE

Delaware has used a Saturday Election Day for local elections and Presidential primaries. Over the past two election cycles, however, the State has moved all primary elections back to the traditional Tuesday Election Day. From 1978 through 2006, local elections, including primaries, were held on Saturdays. The State's first Saturday Presidential primary was in 1996.

Election officials often justify the move to voting during the weekends by claiming an added convenience to voters. In Delaware, Jewish voters did not find it more convenient to vote on Saturdays exclusively. The State's 2002 primary election fell on Rosh Hashanah (the Jewish New Year), and Saturday primaries always coincided with the Jewish Sabbath. In 2004, the Presidential primary was moved to a Tuesday, and, beginning in 2006, the State primary was moved to a Tuesday Election Day.

Administrative Challenges

New Castle County election officials reported that they did not have a problem recruiting enough poll workers. They did note, however, that they were hiring different poll workers for Saturday Election Day than for Tuesday Election Day. Teachers are the most common replacements on Saturday Election Days for traditional Tuesday Election Day poll workers.

Election officials in New Castle County did have a harder time securing enough polling places for Saturday voting. They reported that fewer churches and community centers are available to use as polling places because those facilities are not always available during the weekends.

Voter Turnout

Moving a non-Presidential Federal primary election from Saturday to Tuesday did not appear to substantially affect turnout.

- Tuesday, September 12, 2006: 45.76 percent.
- Saturday, September 7, 2002: 43.42 percent.
- Saturday, September 12, 1998: 37.32 percent.

As reported by local election officials in other States and jurisdictions, election officials in New Castle County reported that voter turnout is directly linked to the candidates and measures on the ballot and not to the day of the week on which the election is conducted.

Conclusion

EAC's study of weekend voting is limited because only a few States allow some form of the alternative voting method and no State is allowed to conduct Federal elections on weekends exclusively. Based on the turnout data in State and local elections from the three States studied, the measurement of voter turnout seems to be affected very little by weekend voting. It is impossible, however, to extrapolate from those turnout data to make predictions about how a move to weekend voting for Federal elections might affect turnout.

The only real certainty is that the cost of administering the election will be higher. Interviews with local election officials reveal that Saturday Election Day usually costs more than Tuesday Election Day. If Congress changes the Federal Tuesday Election Day to 2-day weekend voting, the cost of the election is likely to increase substantially.

With very little data to support a positive effect on turnout and likely higher administrative cost, it is inadvisable at this time for EAC to recommend a move from Tuesday Election Day to weekend voting for Federal elections.

VOTING IN PUERTO RICO

General elections in Puerto Rico for all levels of government coincide with the U.S. Presidential election. The different levels of government are elected using three separate ballots. The first ballot includes the races for Governor and for Resident Commissioner. Although the Federal Resident Commissioner is Puerto Rico's delegate to the U.S. Congress, the race appears on the State ballot. The second ballot is used for choosing members of the Puerto Rico Legislature. The third ballot is used for contests in each of Puerto Rico's 78 municipalities. In Puerto Rico, Election Day is designated as a State holiday.

The Puerto Rico Elections Commission (Comisión Estatal de Elecciones or CEE)—an independent body consisting of a representative of each political party—is responsible for all aspects of election administration in Puerto Rico. In addition to governing traditional voting on Election Day, the CEE governs Puerto Rico's alternative voting methods. This section examines the implementation and effect of Puerto Rico's use of alternative voting methods.

IMPLEMENTATION AND EFFECT

Puerto Rico's election officials use some of the alternative voting methods employed on the U.S. mainland, but they have also used innovative options not established anywhere else in the United States. All of Puerto Rico's alternative voting methods are restricted to specific groups of people. For example, an absentee voter must have a specific excuse—usually related to employment—for voting by absentee ballot. These excuses include employment as a police officer, firefighter, student, and so forth. Puerto Rico also has alternative voting procedures for incarcerated felons, hospitalized individuals, and bedridden voters.

For decades, Puerto Rico has used some of its alternative voting methods, such as absentee voting and early voting. Other methods have been used only in the most recent election in 2004. See Table 7 for the dates of implementation of all of Puerto Rico's alternative voting methods. None of the alternative voting methods in Puerto Rico disrupts Election Day procedures because they are designed to occur before Election Day. Each alternative voting method has restrictive eligibility requirements, which results in most people voting in traditional precinct- based polling places on Election Day.

Territory:	Commonwealth of Puerto Rico
Chief Election Official:	Lic. Ramon E. Gomez Colon, President Puerto Rico Elections Commission 550 Arterial B. Ave. Hato Rey San Juan, PR 0091 9-5552 Phone: 787-777-8675
Number of Registered Voters:	2,178,956 (in 2006)
Alternative Voting Method:	Alternative days, times and places to vote
Implemented:	2004

Table 7. Introduction of Voting Methods in Puerto Rico

Voting Method	Implementation
Absentee and Early Voting	Election law of 1974
Provisional Voting	Decision by the local Supreme Court of 1988 (122 DPR 490)
Prisoner Voting	Decision by Tribunal Special Committee (Junta Revisora) in 1980
Hospital Voting	Elections Commission decision in 2004
Domicile/Bedridden Voting	Elections Commission decision in 2004

Absentee and Early Voting

The CEE must receive all absentee voting requests at least 60 days before the election, and only a small group of citizens is eligible to apply. This group includes active-duty National Guard personnel, Merchant Marines, Department of Labor personnel, members of the diplomatic or foreign aid service, students, commercial airline crews, and essential public servants (e.g., firefighters, police officers, and judges). An eligible voter in one of the preceding categories who is unable to vote in his or her assigned precinct on Election Day may request an absentee ballot and cast the vote by mail.

Puerto Rico also permits some individuals to vote absentee in person before their local elections commissions, usually on the day before Election Day. This process is similar to early voting in some States. Eligible citizens include those individuals working in essential positions on Election Day such as officials of the Correctional Administration (e.g., prison guards), CEE officials, and police officers.

Provisional Voting (Añadidos a Mano)

Since 1988, the CEE has administered a provisional voting and canvassing process called *Añadidos a Mano* (AM). On Election Day, multiple precincts vote in the same polling location. If a voter claims to be registered but does not appear in the precinct's poll book, he or she is permitted to vote in a provisional precinct within the polling place. This provisional precinct is similar to an absentee ballot precinct; no voter is regularly assigned to a provisional precinct, but the votes are tallied there on Election Day for reporting purposes. A voter in a provisional precinct signs an affidavit swearing that he or she is a registered voter in the jurisdiction and casts a ballot, which is placed in an envelope to be verified by CEE staff after Election Day.

Provisional votes must be authenticated before being counted. To safeguard voters' privacy rights and the election's integrity, provisional ballots are kept separate from other ballots when they are sent from the polling places to the local elections commission's office. Provisional ballots that can be authenticated are counted and tallied for the correct precinct. All voters who cast provisional ballots can verify whether their votes were counted by calling a toll-free number or by visiting the local elections commission's office.

Prisoner Voting (Voto de los Con finados)

Since 1980, Puerto Rico has allowed felons and prisoners in State custody to vote. These voters are subject to a two-tier system. If prisoners want to vote in the State, legislative, and municipal elections, they must submit a request in writing using a special absentee voting form at least 60 days before Election Day. If incarcerated voters do not make the request at least 60 days before the election, they may still vote through the AM process. These voters, however, are eligible only for the State ballot and cannot vote in the legislative and municipal elections because they may be incarcerated outside their home jurisdictions and may not have given the CEE enough time to supply the appropriate ballot style.

The CEE conducts penal institution voting on the Sunday before Election Day. Voting on this day allows for sufficient time to transport the votes to the appropriate local elections commissions for adjudication on Election Day. Voting also occurs on Sunday so that it does not interfere with Saturday prison visitation hours.

In the November 2004 election, 5,102 prisoners cast votes. The CEE validated 4,384 of the voters as registered and counted those votes.

Hospital Voting (Voto en Hospitales)

During the general election of 2004, Puerto Rico conducted a pilot program that allowed registered voters who were hospitalized on Election Day to vote outside of their traditional precinct-based polling place. As with some prisoner voting procedures, however, the patients were presented State ballots only and were not permitted to vote in legislative and municipal races, because they may be located outside their home jurisdictions.

It was more difficult for the CEE to determine how to allocate resources for hospital voting than it was for prisoner voting. Patients are much more transient than prisoners and cannot be expected to register their statuses more the 60 days in advance of Election Day. By October 29, 2004, 3 full days before Election Day, each participating hospital's administration submitted to the CEE updated statistics of admitted patients and information about the number of them expected to remain hospitalized on Election Day. The CEE then installed electoral precincts accordingly in public areas inside the hospitals and used mobile precincts for voters who, because of their medical conditions, could not leave their rooms to vote.

Voting in the hospital precincts occurred on the day before the general election. Polls were open during the same hours that traditional precinct-based polling places were open and followed the same procedures that are used on Election Day. Unlike the officials at a regular precinct, however, hospital precinct officials did not count the cast ballots when the polls closed. Instead, after the polls closed, poll workers sent the cast ballots to the corresponding local elections commission's office and then to the CEE's main operations center to be counted along with the ballots cast on Election Day.

The CEE provided hospital voting in approximately 70 hospitals. Hospitalized voters cast 2,673 ballots. The CEE identified 2,438 of those voters as registered and counted their votes.

Domicile/Bedridden Voting (Voto en el Domicilio)

The CEE also conducted a pilot program for bedridden individuals during the 2004 election. Eligible voters with physical impediments, unable to leave their homes on Election Day to vote, could request no later than 45 days before the election, via a person of confidence or the Internet, to vote by this alternative voting method. Unlike hospitalized or prisoner voters, domicile voters were presented ballots for legislative and municipal elections along with the State ballot.

Poll workers carried ballots to those individuals eligible to vote from their homes on the day before Election Day. Votes were cast in the poll worker's presence. Poll workers then certified the cast ballot, sealed it in an envelope, and delivered it to the local elections commission's office to be counted with the votes of its corresponding home precinct on Election Day.

Costs

In Puerto Rico, all poll workers are volunteers representing their respective political parties and are trained by the local elections commissions. Political parties were responsible for selecting and recruiting poll workers who administered Puerto Rico's two pilot programs in 2004. Puerto Rico's election officials were able to keep some costs from rising because they were not recruiting and paying the additional poll workers to conduct hospital and domicile voting. Furthermore, officials reported no noticeable increases in cost to the local elections commissions for registration materials, because most individuals using the alternative voting methods were already registered to vote. Part of the cost associated with the two pilot programs for personnel, training, and administrative expenses was covered by the general election administration budget. The costs associated with absentee and early voting as well as prisoner voting were already included in the general election administration budget.

Additional expenses paid outside the general election administrative budget include the rent for vehicles to transport elections officials to the hospitals or domiciles in which voting took place. and costs to develop, print, and distribute posters and purchase radio and television time to inform voters of the new alternative voting methods. Approximately $70,000 was spent on the information campaign to promote hospital and domicile voting.

Administrative Challenges

The implementation of the prisoner, hospital, and bedridden alternative voting methods did not affect other voting procedures in place on Election Day. To avoid any possible problems, the alternative voting methods were designed to be administered on dates before Election Day. This pre-Election Day method made the administrative challenge of matching legislative and municipal ballots to their appropriate precincts for counting considerably easier.

Most voting in Puerto Rico takes place on the Tuesday Election Day. In 2004, hospital and domicile voting took place 1 day before Election Day, on Monday, November 1. By avoiding weekends during the voting process, there was minimal impact on religious groups. Only prison voting is conducted on a weekend in Puerto Rico. Sunday was chosen to avoid disrupting visitation hours on Saturday.

Voter Turnout

The goal of Puerto Rico's alternative voting methods is to include groups of people in the elections who otherwise could not have voted. Each alternative voting method has a highly restrictive eligibility requirement, which means most of the electorate must still vote on Election Day in traditional precinct-based polling places. Having individuals vote by one of the alternative voting methods could only have resulted in higher overall turnout for the 2004 election than would have been achievable without the options, because those voters would not have been able to vote before the implementation of the various alternative voting methods.

The CEE created an administrative absentee vote board (*Junta de Adminstracion del Voto Ausente*) to manage all absentee voting in Puerto Rico, which includes all its alternative voting methods. The board uses the name and voter identification number (Tarjeta de Identificacion Electoral) on each envelope to verify the voter's eligibility. Ballots from voters whose eligibility cannot be verified are not counted. During the 2004 general election, 22,267 individuals voted by one of the alternative voting methods. Of those ballots, 12,610 were counted; 9,657 ballots were rejected.

The goal of Puerto Rico's alternative voting methods is to include groups of people in the elections who otherwise could not have voted. Each alternative voting method has a highly restrictive eligibility requirement, which means most of the electorate must still vote on Election Day in traditional precinct-based polling places.

CONCLUSION

The CEE is responsible for the design, organization, structure, and supervision of all procedures and practices used in Puerto Rico elections. It is also responsible for periodically evaluating its election procedures and adopting any new alternative voting methods. All new provisions must be approved unanimously by the Puerto Rico Elections Commission members at least 4 months ahead of Election Day.

The CEE did not hastily move from one voting method to another. Instead, the CEE included alternative voting methods to supplement its current precinct-based elections to assist u nderserved groups within the population. It took approximately 6 months to develop and establish the procedures by which the two most recent alternative voting methods were put in place. These innovative practices have been successful to date and could be used in jurisdictions across the United States.

UNIFORM POLL CLOSING

HAVA Section 241 (b)(10) requires a discussion of the "advisability of establishing a uniform poll closing time." A uniform poll closing time would ensure that voters on the west coast are not affected by the announced election returns from the east coast. In some cases, projections have been made about the outcome of the race based on those east coast returns while hours of voting remained in other parts of the country; research shows that knowledge of these projections can influence voters.[64]

Congress has attempted to address the problem of early projections many times. In 1960, Senator Barry Goldwater from Arizona introduced legislation that would have prohibited all media outlets from announcing any election results until after midnight eastern standard time (EST). Although the legislation to limit the ability of the media to make election projections did not make it through Congress, there is another way to combat the controversy regarding election night returns. All polling places in the continental United States could close at the same time.

In 1985, the House of Representatives first passed legislation that would have established a uniform poll closing time, and several bills have been in both the House of Representatives and the Senate as recently as 2002 to do the same. As former Representative Al Swift from

Washington, one of the most ardent proponents of a national uniform poll closing time, has argued, "[a]nything that erodes the integrity of the voting process weakens our democracy. Projecting a Presidential winner before all the polls have closed adversely affects us all, but the problem can be easily solved ..."[65] By closing all polls at the same time, each individual's vote remains free from the outside influence of knowing the outcome.

Among the several different proposals for a federally mandated uniform poll closing, the most common proposals, and the only ones to pass in the House of Representatives, mandate a 9:00 p.m. EST poll closing. They also amend the Uniform Time Act of 1966 to extend daylight saving time in the Pacific Time zone in Presidential election years to the Sunday after Election Day.[66] Other proposals mandate 10:00 p.m. EST poll closing[67] or 11:00 p.m. EST poll closing,[68] and some leave the exact time of uniform poll closing open ended.[69] The most unlikely option floated by some academics would be to establish a single time zone across the country.

The Constitution reserves to the Congress the power to regulate the time, place, and manner for holding Federal elections.[70] A congressional mandate for a 9:00 p.m. EST poll closing would affect the poll closing time in 40 States. Thirty States, mostly in the East, and the District of Columbia would have to extend polling place hours by as many as 3 hours. Nine States in the West would have to reduce polling place hours by as many as 2 hours.[71] Six States in the East would have polling places open for 15 hours and most other eastern States would have them open for 14 hours, while the maximum a western State could reasonably have its polling places open would be for 12 hours.

The States would likely resist any Federal mandate to change polling place hours. Projections of election results in eastern States may affect voters in the West, and it is reasonable to have serious discussions about how to fix the problem. A uniform poll closing, however, is not an advisable solution. Although the alternative voting methods in this report are all intended to expand the ease and convenience of voting, a uniform poll closing would present a huge inconvenience for many voters in the West, who would lose the opportunity to vote after work. Likewise, local election officials in the East would need to keep polls open even longer than they do now. At this time, the negative side effects of a uniform poll closing time are greater than a fix to the early election projection problem.

FEASIBILITY AND ADVISABILITY

The administration of elections is evolving. According to the EAC's 2006 Election Administration and Voting Survey, more than one in five ballots was cast during early and absentee voting during the 2006 midterm elections.[72] As more States move to no-excuse absentee voting and expand early voting, there will likely be a rise in the percentage of ballots cast before Election Day.

Administrative procedures on Election Day itself are also changing. Vote centers enable individuals to vote at many different locations on Election Day instead of a traditional polling place. There are no polling places at all in Oregon because all ballots are cast by mail. Some States consider Election Day to be a holiday and others conduct non-Federal elections on the weekends. The feasibility of the alternative voting methods in this report will be determined by different levels of legislative bodies: local, State, and Federal. The advisability of each of the alternative voting methods in this report varies depending on the jurisdiction. Local and State election officials must take into consideration their jurisdictions' population density, culture of voting, ability to recruit poll workers, and so forth before making any decision to implement a new alternative voting method.

Early Voting

Early voting is traditionally defined as a process by which voters cast their ballots before Election Day at precinct-like polling stations throughout a jurisdiction. Texas has used this process for two decades and other States have been gradually implementing it. The benefits to early voting, as opposed to other convenience voting, include convenience to the voter and security of the ballot. Early voting, however, comes with a high cost, because personnel and facilities must be coordinated for many days in addition to Election Day. Early voting truly is an alternative voting method. It is used mostly by those voters who would alternatively vote on Election Day if it was the only option. Overall, turnout has not significantly increased during the early voting era in Texas. Still, it is advisable for other States to consider the successes of this method of convenience voting.

Election Day Holidays

Some States have declared Election Day State holidays for Federal elections. Advocates of an Election Day Federal holiday often argue that such a holiday would result in higher turnout because individuals would be given the day off from work. Yet, an analysis of the States with Election Day State holidays during Federal elections does not reveal a higher level of turnout. Over the past four Federal elections, the aggregated turnout of States with holidays showed insignificant differences in turnout than States without holidays. The implementation of an Election Day Federal holiday would be accompanied by some costs for the Federal government, because more than 2 million employees would be given a paid day off. It is unclear how many State governments and private businesses would close as a result of the Federal holiday, which advocates say results in more convenience for voters. Finally, it is unlikely that a Federal holiday would positively affect voter turnout when a State holiday does not. Until more research can be completed about the positive effects of Election Day holidays to counter the inevitable drawback of higher administrative cost, it is inadvisable at this time to establish a legal public holiday on the Federal Election Day.

Vote-by-Mail

Absentee voting has been around since the Civil War. It was originally intended for soldiers who were away from home on Election Day. Today, absentee voting has expanded to all States, of which 31 allow no-excuse absentee voting for all individuals.[73] Oregon has moved one step further and created an all vote-by-mail system. Officials there claim clear benefits for both local election officials and voters.

Election officials do not need polling places or poll workers in a vote-by-mail system. Voter registration lists tend to be more accurate because the frequent mailing of nonforwardable ballots provides updated information on the actual home addresses of voters. Furthermore, some evidence supports the supposition that vote-by-mail elections might be less costly to administer than precinct-based elections and may increase turnout. Voters have the convenience of voting from home and can choose to mail the ballot back to the election office or drop it off at conveniently located sites around the jurisdiction. Although Oregon has additional concerns about ballot integrity, the State believes it has solved the problem with its 100 percent signature match procedures. This alternative voting method works well in Oregon, which already had a history of higher than average absentee voting. Officials in other jurisdictions considering a move to a vote-by-mail method are advised to evaluate the current methods of voting that their citizens use most before instituting any changes to their election systems.

Vote Centers

Even the traditional precinct-based election is evolving. There was a time when the poll workers knew all the voters in their given precincts. In smaller jurisdictions with smaller precincts, this is still sometimes the case. As precincts have become larger, however, the administration of elections has become less of a neighbor-to-neighbor experience. Small neighborhood precincts often are not the most convenient places for individuals to vote today, because the voters are not near their residences as much during normal polling place hours. First attempted in Colorado, vote centers are an alternative voting method in which individuals choose to vote in any one of larger, strategically located polling sites throughout the county on Election Day. This added convenience for voters has been well received, and local election administrators enjoy the benefits of economies of scale. Only two Federal elections have been conducted with vote centers, however, and it is unclear to what extent vote centers can be credited with raising overall turnout (including absentee and early voting) when voter turnout on the actual Election Day declined after the change from traditional precincts to vote centers. Jurisdictions interested in vote centers are advised to consider all the planning that Colorado did before implementing vote centers and to look at the data on voter turnout and administrative costs after the 2008 Presidential election in jurisdictions using vote centers.

Weekend Voting

Federal law requires that elections for Federal office occur on the first Tuesday after the first Monday in November. Yet, the traditional Tuesday Election Day is predicated on the needs of an agrarian society and may not still be the most optimal day on which Americans should vote. Weekend voting as an alternative voting method might provide more convenience to voters and increase voter turnout, although election officials' experiences with some State and local elections conducted on the weekends have shown some drawbacks in recruiting poll workers and finding appropriate polling place locations, as well as pushback from religious groups. With very little data to support a positive effect on turnout and likely

60 U.S. Election Assistance Commission

higher administrative costs, it is inadvisable at this time for EAC to recommend a move from Tuesday Election Day to weekend voting for Federal elections.

Voting in Puerto Rico

Puerto Rico has been very innovative with its system of election administration. Some of Puerto Rico's alternative voting methods, such as absentee voting and early voting, have been used for decades. Others have been used only in the most recent elections in 2004. None of the alternative voting methods in Puerto Rico disrupts Election Day procedures, because they were designed to occur before Election Day. Each alternative voting method has highly restrictive eligibility requirements, which results in voting by most people in traditional precinct-based polling places on Election Day. Specifically, programs are in place for prisoner voting, hospital voting, and domicile/bedridden voting. The EAC recommends further research into how some of these unique programs could be implemented in other jurisdictions.

End Notes

[1] 42 U.S.C. § 15321 (2006).

[2] § 15381(b)(10) (2006).

[3] United States. Cong. House. Committee on Energy and Commerce. Subcommittee on Elections. Alternative Ballot Techniques. Hearing, 22 Sept. 1994. 103rd Cong., 2nd sess. Washington: GPO, 1994.

[4] Ibid.

[5] Texas. Committee on Elections, Texas House of Representatives. Interim Report to the 71st Texas Legislature. Austin: The Committee [1988]. pp. 3-6.

[6] Texas. Committee on Elections, Texas House of Representatives. Interim Report 1992. Austin: The Committee [1992]. pp. 5-8.

[7] Tex. Elec. Code Ann. § 85.062 (2003).

[8] Ibid.

[9] Tex. Elec. Code Ann. § 85.067 (2003).

[10] The National Voter Registration Act of 1993, also known as Motor Voter, went into effect on January 1, 1995. Although the law improved access to voter registration and information, it made it more difficult for jurisdictions to remove voters from the voter registration list. With the added difficulty of removing voters from the list, it is not surprising that the turnout of registered voters has declined in certain elections since 1995.

[11] The Voting Integrity Project, Inc. et al v. Elton Bomer, 199 F.3d 773 (5th Cir. 2000).

[12] Miguel Hernanez Chapter of the Am. GI Forum v. Bexar County, No. SA-03CA-816-RF (W.D. Tex. August 28, 2003).

[13] Ibid.

[14] Ibid.

[15] 42 U.S.C. § 1973c (2006).

[16] "2006 Polling Place Hours by State." Chart. National Association of Secretaries of State. Nov. 2006. 14 Jul 2008 <http://nass.org/index.php?option=com_content&task=view&id =71&Itemid=21 7>.

[17] Cong. Rec. 7 May 1992: E1297.

[18] United States. Bureau of Labor Statistics, U.S. Department of Labor. Career Guide to Industries, 2008-09 Edition, Federal Government, Excluding the Postal Service. [Washington, DC :] BLS, 2008. 14 July 2008 <http://www.bls.gov/oco/cg/cgs041.htm>.
United States. Bureau of Labor Statistics, U.S. Department of Labor. Occupational Outlook Handbook, 2008-09 Edition. [Washington, DC :] BLS, 2008. 19 August 2008 <http://www. bls.gov/oco/ocos141.htm>.

[19] United States. Cong. House. Statistics of the Presidential and Congressional Election of November 5, 1940. 15 Jan. 1941. 77th Cong., 1st sess. Washington: 1941. 14 Jul. 2008 <http:// clerk.house.gov/member_info/electionInfo/1940election.pdf>.

[20] United States. Bureau of the Census, U.S. Department of Commerce. Current Population Reports Population Estimates. [Washington, DC :] Bureau of the Census, 1948. 14 July 2008 <http://www.census.gov/population>.

[21] Ibid.

[22] Voter turnout figures were derived from the number of votes cast for the highest office and the voting age population (VAP), as reported by Dr. Michael McDonald and the United States Election Project. 17 Jul. 2008 <httpi/elections.gmu.edu/voterjurnout.htm>.

[23] Adapted from "A Brief History of Vote by Mail." Chart. Oregon Secretary of State. 14 Jul 2008 <http://www.sos.state.or.us/ elections/vbm/history.html>.

[24] Oregon. Senate. Senate Bills Vetoed by Governor after Adjournment 1995 Regular Session. Salem: The Senate [1995]. 14 Jul 2008 <http://www.leg.state svetocal.txt>.

[25] 1981 Or. Laws Ch. 805.

[26] 1983 Or. Laws Ch. 199 Sec. 1.

[27] "A Brief History of Vote by Mail." Chart. Oregon Secretary of State. 14 Jul 2008 <http://www.sos.state history.html>.

[28] 1987 Or. Laws Ch. 357 Sec. 4.

[29] "A Brief History of Vote by Mail." Chart. Oregon Secretary of State. 14 Jul 2008 <http://www.sos.state history.html>.

[30] "Official Participation Summary by County Special U.S. Senate General Election January 30, 1996." Chart. Oregon Secretary of State. 14 Jul 2008 <http://www.sos.state.or.us/ elections/jan3096/other.info/brsum.htm>.

[31] Oregon. Senate. Senate Bills Vetoed by Governor after Adjournment 1995 Regular Session. Salem: The Senate [1995]. 14 Jul 2008 <http://www.leg.state>.

[32] Oregon. Senate. Senate Bills. Salem: The Senate [1995]. 14 Jul 2008 <http://www.leg.state>.

[33] "Official County Participation Summary Oregon Presidential Preference Primary March 12, 1996." Chart. Oregon Secretary of State. 14 Jul 2008 <http://www.sos.state mar1296/other.info/coparsum.htm>.

[34] "Official Voter Participation Statistics May 19, 1998 Biennial Primary." Chart. Oregon Secretary of State. 14 Jul 2008 <http:// www.sos.state>.

[35] "Official Results November 3, 1998 General Election State Measure 60." Chart. Oregon Secretary of State. 14 Jul 2008 <http://www.sos.state. htm>.

[36] Oregon. Secretary of State. Vote By Mail Procedures Manual. Salem: Secretary of State [2008]. 14 Jul 2008 <http://www.sos. state>.

[37] "Measure No. 60." Oregon Secretary of State. 14 Jul 2008 <http://www.sos.state m60.htm>.

[38] Compiled from Oregon revised statutes, administrative rules, and vote-by-mail procedures.

[39] "Ballot Return History 1996 General Election to Current." Chart. Oregon Secretary of State. 14 Jul 2008 <http://www.sos. state>.

[40] Marion County (Oregon). Audio Voter Pamphlet. [Salem, Oregon:] Department of Elections [2008]. 14 Jul 2008 <http:// www.co.marion.or.us/CO/elections/may2008avp.htm>.

[41] Oregon. Secretary of State. "Last Day to Safely Mail Ballot is Here." Press Release. 3 November 2006. 14 Jul 2008 <http:// www.sos.state>.

[42] "Official Election Participation Statistics November 5, 1996 Biennial General Election." Chart. Oregon Secretary of State. 14 Jul 2008 <http://www.sos.state. info/totbycty.htm>.

[43] "2000 General Election Statistical Summary." Chart. Oregon Secretary of State. 14 Jul 2008 <http://www.sos.state.or.us/ elections/nov72000/other.info/genstats.pdf>.

[44] "Statistical Summary 2004 General Election." Chart. Oregon Secretary of State. 14 Jul 2008 <http://www.sos.state.or.us/elections/nov22004/g04stats.pdf>.

[45] "2000 General Election Statistical Summary." Chart. Oregon Secretary of State. 14 Jul 2008 <http://www.sos.state.or.us/ elections/nov72000/other.info/genstats.pdf>.

[46] "Statistical Summary 2004 General Election." Chart. Oregon Secretary of State. 14 Jul 2008 <http://www.sos.state.or.us/ elections/nov22004/g04stats.pdf>.

[47] The Voting Integrity Project, Inc. et al v. Phil Keisling, Secretary of State of Oregon, 259 F.3d 1169, 1176 (9th Cir. 2001).

[48] Southwell, Priscilla L. "Final Report, Survey of Vote-ByMail Senate Election." Presented to the Vote-by-Mail Citizen Commission, Oregon, 3 Apr. 1996. 14 Jul 2008 <https:// scholarsbank.uoregon.edu/dspace/bitstream/1794/1268/5/ VBM+Full+Report.pdf>.

[49] Michael W. Traugott and Robert G. Mason. "Preliminary report on the characteristics of the Oregon electorate participating in the special general election for the U.S. Senate on January 30, 1996." Technical report, University of Michigan and Oregon State University, 30 May 1996.

[50] Magelby, David. "An Initial Assessment of Oregon's Voteby-Mail." Presented to the Vote-by-Mail Citizen Commission, Oregon, 3 Apr. 1996.

[51] University of Pennsylvania. Fels Institute of Government. "MyVote1 National Election Report: Voice of the Electorate 2006." [Philadelphia, PA :] Penn, 2007. pp. 6. 15 July 2008 <http://www. fels.upenn.edu/Projects/myvote1_report_8_20_07.pdf>.

52 1 Colorado Revised Statutes § 5-102.7.

53 http://www.larimer.org/elections

54 United States. Department of Justice. Americans with Disabilities Act ADA Checklist for Polling Places. [Washington, DC:] DOJ, 2004. 15 Jul 2008 <http://www.ada.gov/votingprt.pdf>.

55 According to counties implementing vote centers (in their comments to Larimer County Clerk Scott Doyle)

56 Denver (Colorado). Election Commission Investigative Panel: Findings and Recommendations. [Denver, Colo.:] The City [December 2006].

57 Ibid.

58 Stein, Robert M. and Greg Vonnahme. "Election Day Vote Centers and Voter Turnout." Prepared for presentation at the 2006 Annual Meetings of the Midwest Political Science Association, Chicago, IL, April 20-23. 15 Jul 2008 <http://www3.brookings.edu/gs/projects/ electionreform/ 20060418Stein.pdf>.

59 S. 2638, 110th Cong. (2008).

60"Absentee and Early Voting Laws." Chart. The Early Voting Information Center at Reed College. Feb. 2008. 15 Jul 2008 < http://www.earlyvoting.net/states>.

61 18 Louisiana Revised Statutes § 533.

62"State Wide Post Election Statistical Report Election Date 11/07/2000." Chart. Louisiana Secretary of State Elections Division. 15 Jul 2008 <http://www400.sos.louisiana.gov/stats/Post_Election_Statistics/ Statewide/2000_ 1 107_sta.txt>.
"State Wide Post Election Statistical Report for Election of 11/02/2004." Chart. Louisiana Secretary of State Elections Division. 15 Jul 2008 <http://www400.sos.louisiana.gov/stats/Post_Election_Statistics/ Statewide/2004_ 1 102_sta.txt>.

63"State Wide Post Election Statistical Report Election Date 11/17/2007." Chart. Louisiana Secretary of State Elections Division. 15 Jul 2008 <http://www400.sos.louisiana.gov/stats/Post_Election_Statistics/ Statewide/2007_ 11 17_sta.pdf>.
"State Wide Post Election Statistical Report for Election of 11/15/2003." Chart. Louisiana Secretary of State Elections Division. 15 Jul 2008 <http://www400.sos.louisiana.gov/stats/Post_Election_Statistics/ Statewide/2003_ 11 15_sta.txt>.
"State Wide Post Election Statistical Report for Election of 11/20/1999." Chart. Louisiana Secretary of State Elections Division. 15 Jul 2008 <http://www400.sos.louisiana.gov/stats/Post_Election_Statistics/ Statewide/1999_ 1 120_sta.txt>.

64 Crespin, Michael H. and Ryan J. Vander Wielen. "The Influence of Media Projections on Voter Turnout In Presidential Elections from 1980-2000." Prepared for presentation at the 2002 Annual Meeting of the Midwest Political Science Association. pp. 2-3.
Jackson, John E. "Election Night Reporting and Voter Turnout." American Journal of Political Science 27.4 (November 1983): 615-635. pp. 633.

65 Swift, Al. Letter. New York Times. 20 Dec. 1988. 11 Jul. 2008 <http://query 3BF933A 15751C1A96E948260>.

66 H.R. 3525, 99th Cong. (1986); S. 628, 10 1st Cong. (1989); H.R. 18, 10 1st Cong. (1989); H.R. 1554, 103rd Cong. (1993); S. 3287, 1 06th Cong. (2000); H.R 5678, 106th Cong. (2000); and, S. 50, 107th Cong. (2001).

67 S. 136, 10 1st Cong. (1989); S. 571, 1 05th Cong. (1997); and, S. 175, 107th Cong. (2001).

68 H.R. 3153, 1 05th Cong. (1998); H.R. 668, 106th Cong. (1999); and, H.R. 1666, 107th Cong. (2001).

69 H.R. 96, 10 1st Cong. (1989).

70 U.S. Constitution. Article I, Section 4 and Article II, Section 1.

71 "2006 Polling Place Hours by State." Chart. National Association of Secretaries of State. Nov. 2006. 11 Jul 2008 <http://nass.org/index.php?option=com_content&task=view&id =71&Itemid=21 7>.

72United States. U.S. Election Assistance Commission. The 2006 Election Administration and Voting Survey. Washington: EAC, 2007. 11 Jul. 2008 <http://www.eac.gov/files/Eds2006/ eds2006/edsr-final-adopted-version.pdf>. pp. 14.

73"Absentee and Early Voting Laws." Chart. The Early Voting Information Center at Reed College. Feb. 2008. 11 Jul 2008 <http://www.earlyvoting.net/states>.

In: Voting Alternatives, Hotlines and Websites
Editors: Sean M. Thomas, and Daniel P. Allton

ISBN: 978-1-61324-593-4
© 2011 Nova Science Publishers, Inc.

Chapter 2

VOTER HOTLINE STUDY

U.S. Election Assistance Commission

EXECUTIVE SUMMARY

The telephone remains a primary communication tool between election offices and the customers they serve—America's voters. Election officials nationwide use a variety of tools to provide information to stakeholders. From answering routine questions on Election Day to providing poll worker training and assignment information and responding to inquiries on the status of provisional ballots and general voter complaints and concerns, the outcome of this study reiterates the importance of providing fast, efficient, and accurate election information.

Prevalence of Dedicated Phone Banks

Election officials are investing in a variety of methods to manage the influx of calls and requests for information on peak election days, including 24-hour automated telephone banks and personalized, live telephone operators. However, only about 1 in 20 (5 percent) election offices in the United States that admin-ister or oversee Federal elections have a dedicated phone hotline expressly for the purpose of communicating with voters and/or poll workers. State-level elec-tion offices were the most likely to have used dedicated phone hotlines in the 2006 election season. Thirteen of the 27 (48 percent) State election offices that responded to the 2007 survey of election officials conducted for this study said they operated a voter and/or poll worker hotline.

Dedicated phone hotlines were much less common among county-level offices. Just short of one in 10 county-level offices said they used hotlines. And only a handful of election offices in cities or townships (1 percent) utilized a dedicated phone hotline to provide information to voters and/or poll workers in 2006.

The survey, in which 1,466 election officials participated, revealed that larger election offices are more likely to have used a dedicated phone hotline in the 2006 election season than are smaller offices. Offices that report having a dedi-cated hotline employ between 3 and 22 full-time staff and from 1 to 10 part-time staff. By contrast, offices that did not have a dedicated hotline are much smaller and are typically staffed by 1 to 3 full-time and 1 to 3 part-time staff. Similarly, election jurisdictions that serve large numbers of voters are more likely than smaller jurisdictions to report using a dedicated phone hotline. The median voter population of offices that used hotlines in the 2006 election season is roughly 185,500, with the number of voters typically varying between 29,000 and 575,000. By comparison, jurisdictions that did not operate hotlines are much smaller—typically serving between 1,300 and 20,000 voters with a median voter population of approximately 6,100.

Diversifying the Response Tools

Conversations with and survey responses from more than 1,466 election offices across the country reveal that communication tools and techniques are changing. Many State and local jurisdictions are supplementing the traditional telephone banks and toll-free access lines with Web sites, text messaging, and pod casting. Recognizing the diversity of the voting population, many offices are using a combination of one or more of the above tools.

Services Provided via Phone

The survey revealed that most election offices with hotlines are providing infor-mation on the most frequent voter queries: "Am I registered?" and "Where do I go to vote?" Three-quarters or more of hotlines directly offered information to voters on whether or not the voter is currently registered (79 percent) or information on the voter's voting location and the polling hours in the voter's polling place (77 percent).

Jurisdictions with dedicated hotlines report that the bulk of the calls they receive have to do with issues with where to go to vote (42 percent) or checking on registration status (33 percent). Jurisdictions report that fewer than 2 in 10 calls are about receipt of absentee ballots (8 percent), general nonfraud complaints (6 percent) or fraud-related concerns (1 percent).

Development and Costs of Hotlines

More than 8 in 10 jurisdictions with dedicated hotlines report that the process of developing the hotline was easy, and two-thirds reported that they had devel-oped them in house, usually with support from the county or State technology department.

Sampling of Successful Practices

Election officials who participated in the survey provided some tips for devel-oping and enhancing automated phone systems. Researchers also followed up with a number of election officials to gather some successful practices, including ideas for tracking the types and number of incoming calls, as well as for supple-menting the services provided by phone systems.

SECTION ONE: ABOUT THE STUDY

The focus of the 2007 U.S. Election Assistance Commission (EAC)-commissioned survey of election officials and report on government-sponsored voter hotlines was to gather information and provide assistance to election officials who are seeking to start up or improve their phone services. The bulk of the ques-tions asked in an extensive survey of election officials originated from the EAC in its Statement of Work. The EAC contractors, The Pollworker Institute and the International Foundation for Election Systems (FES) worked with the EAC research director to modify the questions to make them user friendly for jurisdic-tions taking the survey.

Originally, the EAC limited the definition of voter hotline to toll-free numbers. However, the EAC later agreed that the definition be broadened so that data could be collected from government agencies that employ non-toll-free phone systems to provide services to voters and pollworkers and to receive information from callers. The resulting survey reflected this updated definition.

SECTION TWO: ABOUT THE DATA

This report contains the results of a Web-based survey sent to Federal, State, and local-level offices that administer and/or oversee Federal elections. Invitations to complete the survey were sent to a total of 5,920 election offices, including 3 Federal agencies, 50 State election directors and their counterparts in Puerto Rico and the District of Columbia, and 5,868 local-level (countys, citys, and township) jurisdictions.

Jurisdictions were sent invitations to complete the survey by e-mail or fax, depending on the information available. About two-thirds of the offices were sent a link by e-mail; the remaining one-third were sent a fax with the information needed to log on to the survey. An invitation to take the survey was not sent to 316 offices for which we were not able to obtain an e-mail address or fax number; in most cases we were able to confirm that the election office in question had neither e-mail nor a fax machine.

Out of the roughly 6,184 local-level election jurisdictions in the 50 U.S. States, invitations to complete the survey were sent to a total of 5,868 local-level election offices. In States in which election duties are divided among more than one office (such as a county clerk and a registrar of voters), the invitation was sent to the office that handles the bulk of voters' questions and voter communication. The survey invitation was sent to the head of this office with directions that the survey should be completed by the person in the office most knowledgeable about voter communication, especially phone hotlines or phone-based voter information efforts. In this way, this survey contains only one response per election jurisdiction. (Note that in the State of New York the Board of Elections has two commissioners—one Democratic and one Republican. In order to maintain the principle of one response per jurisdiction, we used a random selection method so that in half of the counties/ boroughs the survey was sent to the Republican commissioner and in half to the Democratic commissioner.)

Jurisdictions had between August 28 and September 17, 2007, to complete the online survey, and election offices were contacted up to five times, including with an introductory letter, an invitation to join the survey, and three reminders encouraging their participation.

Readers are reminded that this was an online survey, and thus the lack of Internet access in some smaller jurisdictions may have depressed participation, although we know that election officials in some of these jurisdictions took the survey from their home computers and a small handful called in to take the survey by phone with one of the project researchers.

In total, 1,466 election offices took the survey—1 Federal agency, 27 State election offices, 1,438 local-level offices—resulting in a 25 percent response rate. Broken down by region, the survey was completed by 29 percent of election jurisdictions in the West, 25 percent in the South, 23 percent in the Northeast, and 23 percent in the Midwest.

SECTION THREE. PREVALENCE OF HOTLINES

Minority of Election Offices Use Phone Hotlines to Communicate with Voters and/or Poll Workers

The majority (63 percent) of election offices did not operate phone hotlines to communicate with voters and/or poll workers in their communities during the 2006 election season. A little more than one-third of election offices report that they used phone-based information lines to communicate with voters and/or poll workers in their area, but for most offices, this phone hotline was the same as their office's main number. Only about 1 in 20 (5 percent) election offices in the United States that administer or oversee Federal elections have a dedicated phone hotline expressly for the purpose of communicating with voters and/or poll workers.

Did your office operate a phone-based information line, phone bank, or "hotline" to provide services or information to voters or poll workers in your area?

Yes, had hotline as a dedicated phone number **5%**
Yes, had hotline same as office main number **32%**
No, no hotline **63%**

State Election Offices Most Likely to Have Dedicated Hotlines

When considering the different types of election offices surveyed, State-level election offices are the most likely to have used dedicated phone hotlines in the 2006 election season. Thirteen of the 27 (48 percent) State election offices that responded to the survey said they operated a voter and/or poll worker hotline.

Dedicated phone hotlines were much less common among county-level offices. Just short of 1 in 10 county-level offices said they used hotlines, and only a handful of election offices in cities or townships (1 percent) utilized a dedicated phone hotline to provide information to voters and/or poll workers in 2006.

Hotlines by Level of Government

	Federal	State	County	City / Township
No, no hotline	0 (–%)	5 (19%)	352 (46%)	563 (83%)
Yes, had hotline same as office main number	1 (–%)	9 (33%)	351 (46%)	108 (16%)
Yes, had hotline as a dedicated phone number	0 (–%)	13 (48%)	57 (8%)	7 (1%)
Total jurisdictions reporting	1 (100%)	27 100%)	760 100%)	678 (100%)

Offices with More Staff and Large Voter Populations are More Likely to Utilize Hotlines

In a similar vein, the survey revealed that larger election offices are more likely to have used a dedicated phone hotline in the 2006 election season than are smaller offices. Offices that report having a dedicated hotline employ between 3 and 22 full-time staff and from 1 to 10 part-time staff. By contrast, offices that did not have a dedicated hotline are much smaller and are typically staffed by 1 to 3 fulltime and 1 to 3 part-time staff.

How many full-time and part-time staff work in your election office? Approximately how many voters are in your jurisdiction?			
	1st Quartile	Median	3rd Quartile
Offices with dedicated hotlines			
Number of full-time staff	3	8	22
Number of part-time staff	1	2	10
Number of voters in jurisdiction	29,000	185,000	575,000
Offices without dedicated hotlines			
Number of full-time staff	1	2	3
Number of part-time staff	1	1	3
Number of voters in jurisdiction	1,300	6,000	20,000

Likewise, election jurisdictions that serve large numbers of voters are more likely than smaller jurisdictions to report using a dedicated phone hotline. Election jurisdictions will require a certain number of telephones and phone lines to maintain a useful toll-free telephone service and avoid the busy signal or dump-to-voice-mail problem.

"In a major election our call centers field more than 10,000 calls per hour. The volume outmatches our capacity of operators, phones, and computers. Our 1-800 numbers are critically important in that the automated func-tions allow us to immediately respond to the bulk of the calls on issues such as where to vote and registration confirmation. This leaves our skilled operators available for those calls that require a live interaction."

Dean Logan, Los Angeles County Acting Registrar-Recorder/County Clerk

The survey revealed that the median voter population of offices that used hotlines in the 2006 election season is roughly 185,500, with the number of voters typically varying between 29,000 and 575,000. By comparison, jurisdictions that did not operate hotlines are much smaller—typically serving between 1,300 and 20,000 voters with a median voter population of approximately 6,100.

Was the information line or "hotline" the same as your office's main number or did you have a phone number dedicated specifically to providing information to voters and/or pollworkers?				
	Northeast	**Midwest**	**South**	**West**
Offices with dedicated hotlines	10 (3%)	13 (2%)	36 (10%)	18 (15%)
Total jurisdictions reporting	393 (100%)	602 (100%)	349 (100%	121 (100%)

Hotlines Most Prevalent in the West and South

Phone-based hotlines are most prevalent in election jurisdictions located in the western and southern States of the country. More than 1 in 10 election jurisdictions in the West (15 percent) and South (10 percent) report having used a phone-based hotline during the 2006 election season. By contrast, fewer than 1 in 20 jurisdictions in the Northeast (3 percent) or Midwest (2 percent) say they have a hotline.

The relatively high reliance of hotlines in the West and the South is almost certainly a function of the size of election jurisdictions in those regions—phone-based hotlines dedicated solely to providing information to voters are simply not needed in smaller jurisdictions where the call volumes can easily be handled by the main, all-purpose office number. According to the 2004 EAC Election Day Survey, jurisdictions in the West and South are many times larger than those in the Midwest and Northeast. The median number of voting-aged citizens in western election jurisdictions is approximately 16,006 and is 19,157 in the South. By comparison, the median number of voting-aged citizens in the Northeast is roughly 2,644 and is 1,397 in the Midwest. Furthermore, a large percentage of jurisdictions in the Northeast (15 percent) and Midwest (21 percent) are "micro" districts that serve populations of fewer than 500 voting-aged citizens. Very few election jurisdic-tions in the West (1 percent) and South (.2 percent) serve fewer than 500 citi

Paraphrasing the words of one election official in a microsized jurisdiction in Wisconsin:

We don't need a hotline. If someone has a question, they just walk into the office and ask me.

Increasing Reliance on Web Sites to Serve Voters

Election offices nationwide are turning to the Internet to provide Web-based customer service. Through discussions with election officials, it is apparent that offices across the country have realized that the initial cost to develop and launch a Web site pays off in the long run because voters are able to get answers to a variety of questions at any time of the day, on any day of the week.

> "We don't have a hotline per se....rather we use our website to interface with the majority of our voters and that has worked extremely well."
>
> Gary Smith, Forsyth County, Georgia

Web sites are open 24 hours a day, 7 days a week. Voters have the freedom of "visiting the election office" from the comfort of their own homes. More and more election offices are providing resource tools on their Web Sites, enabling voters to confirm their voter registration status, find their polling place and print a map, and review and print their sample ballot. These services, along with the ability to learn how to use voting equipment, access online poll worker training tools, and e-mail questions to the election official, are all examples of how the Internet-based services in election offices are improving communication and expanding the level of customer service provided to voters nationwide.

Text-messaging and pod-casting services provide election officials instant communication techniques and links to voters. Fortunately, these services are often those utilized by the 18 to 35-year-old population—a segment of the voting population that continues to be targeted in voter outreach efforts. Imagine a voting popula-tion with cell phones receiving text messages that say, "The polls are now open for voting. Click on this link to find your polling place location." This puts customer service at the fingertips of all voters and at the same time alleviates the backlog of phone calls at Election Central on Election Day.

SECTION FOUR: FEATURES OF HOTLINES

Majority of Hotlines are Operated on Normal Toll Phone Lines

The majority of dedicated phone hotlines in operation during the 2006 election season operated on normal, toll-call phone lines. Seven in 10 (71 percent) responding jurisdictions say that their hotlines operated on a normal toll-call basis. Nearly one-half of jurisdictions (47 percent) said they operated a toll-free hotline with 19 percent of jurisdictions saying their office offered both a toll-free and a normal toll-call hotline.

All of the 13 State-level election offices responding operated a toll-free hotline, with a couple of States also offering a normal toll-call hotline. In contrast, among county-level and city and township election offices, there is an almost equal split in the utilization of toll-free versus toll-call hotlines, with a small tendency to opt to use toll-call rather than toll-free hotline numbers.

Was this information hotlne toll-free or a normal toll-call hotline?		
	Toll Free	Toll Call
	%	%
All jurisdictions	47	71
States	100	8
Local jurisdictions	36	46

Most Hotlines Open all Day or during Polling Hours on Election Day

The plurality of jurisdictions (47 percent) operate their hotlines 24 hours on Election Day and most of the rest have their hotlines in operation roughly the same hours that the polls are open in their area (41 percent). Only a little more than 1 in 10 offices keep their hotlines open during normal office hours (11 percent) or extended office hours (1 percent).

Please indicate when, if at all, your information line(s) or "hotline(s) are in operation".			
	Election Day	Election Season (Excluding Election Day	Remainder of the Year
	%	%	%
24 hours	47	24	21
When polls are open (approx.)	41	—	—
Extended office Hours	1	4	0
Normal office Hours	11	53	53
Not in operation	0	20	26

During the rest of the election season, however, only about one-fourth of hotlines (24 percent) operate 24-hours. Instead, a little more than one-half (53 percent) operate within normal office hours or extended office hours (4 percent). And 20 percent of the hotlines in operation during the 2006 election season were in operation only on Election Day.

The remainder of the year outside of election season, only about one in five hotlines (21 percent) are in operation 24 hours, while roughly one-half are in operation during normal office hours (53 percent) and one-fourth (26 percent) are not in operation at all.

SECTION FIVE: INFORMATION AVAILABLE TO CALLERS

Calls from Voters

Telephones remain a valuable tool in communicating with voters, especially those voters who do not use or do not have ready access to a computer. Telephones can be a useful two-way dialog, as opposed to a one-sided message emanating from an election jurisdiction.

Telephone lines can be a first-line form of communication with election jurisdictions that do not have Web sites or the capacity to "snail-mail" voting information. Even for jurisdictions that have advanced Web sites, Web portals and extensive voter mailings (e.g., sample ballot booklets), hotlines can be an invaluable way for election officials to get real-time feedback from voters, such as to report the status of a polling place (e.g., "the polling place I am assigned to is not open") or to report a problem with an incorrectly drawn precinct boundary line.

We asked jurisdictions whether different types of information were directly available to voters through their jurisdiction's hotline or, if not directly available, whether the hotline had provisions for transferring that person to the appropriate person or office. For each type of information asked about, nearly all hotlines either provided the information directly through the hotline or referred the caller to the appropriate person or office.

More specifically, three-fourths or more of hotlines directly offered information to voters on legal deadlines to request and return absentee ballots (81 percent), whether the voter is currently registered (79 percent), or the voter's voting location and the polling hours in the voter's polling place (77 percent).

Further, roughly 6 in 10 or more of jurisdictions report that their hotlines directly provided information on the voting system used in the voter's polling place (65 percent), general complaints and concerns (63 percent), clarification of laws and/or procedures (61 percent), request or check status of absentee ballot (60 percent), information on accessibility provisions in polling locations for voters with disabilities (60 percent), or how to become a poll worker (59 percent). Most of the rest of the jurisdictions that did not provide this information directly through their hotline said that their hotline had a provision for referring callers with these information needs to the appropriate person or office.

Please indicate if the service is available to voters through your office's hotline(s).			
	Ava Available Through Hotline	Not Available but Hotline Refers Caller to Appropriate Person/Office	Not Available and Hotline Does Not Refer Caller
	%	%	%
Information on legal deadlines to request/return absentee ballot	81	15	4
Voter registration— am I registered?	79	16	4
Information on voting location and hours	77	18	4
Information on voting system used in voter's polling place	65	25	8
Other general voter complaints/concerns	63	33	4
Clarification of laws and/or procedures	61	32	5
Request or check status of absentee ballot	60	34	5
Information on accessibility provisions in polling locations for voters with disabilities	60	33	5
How to be a poll worker	58	36	5
Provisional ballot status	55	40	5
Voter information specific to overseas and military voters—UOCAVA ballot sent, received (status)	55	38	7
Report fraud—file HAVA complaint	51	42	5

Slim majorities of jurisdictions provide information via hotlines on provisional ballot status (55 percent), voter information specific to Uniformed and Overseas Citizen Absentee Voting Act (UOCAVA) ballot sent/received status (55 percent), or reporting fraud and/or filing a Help America Vote Act (HAVA) complaint (51 percent). Again, almost all of those jurisdictions that did not offer the information directly through their hotline were able to transfer the call to the appropriate person or office to assist the caller. In particular, in at least one State, calls to the election office regarding the status of a provisional ballot are referred to the State election office.

Communicating with Poll Workers

In addition to providing services to voters, many hotlines are used for communicating with poll workers. Nearly three-fourths (71 percent) of jurisdictions use hotlines as a way of communicating with their poll workers to clarify laws and/or procedures or troubleshoot problems at the polls on Election Day. Almost as many jurisdictions also use hotlines to communicate with poll workers on these issues prior to Election Day, and more than one-half (57 percent) of jurisdictions provide information on poll worker recruiting and deployment via their hotlin

One-fourth (25 percent) of jurisdictions report that they use their hotline for poll workers to signal the opening and closing of individual polling places, while 30 percent refer calls of this nature to the appropriate person or office. However, a large number of jurisdictions (44 percent) neither use hotlines directly to signal the opening and closing of polling stations nor refer hotline callers on this issue to another office.

Majority of Hotlines Operate Solely in English, but Many Offer Support in an Alternative Language

Hotlines can be a very important tool for voters with limited English proficiency. Election offices are increasingly identifying staff who possess the language capacity to assist such voters and/or off site resources to provide such services. An example of such a system is the Los Angeles County 1–800–481–8683 Multilingual Assistance Hotline. Voters can call this toll-free number to request translated voter registration forms, translated sample ballot booklets, translated voting instructions, etc., and to locate their polling place. To obtain assistance in his or her language, the voter asks to speak with an interpreter who serves as a liaison between the voter and the election information staff.

Three in 10 jurisdictions (30 percent) offer some sort of alternative language support with Spanish being the most often offered language. Roughly one-fourth (26 percent) of responding jurisdictions report that they offer Spanish language services through their hotline. A few jurisdictions also offer Chinese (7 percent), Tagalog (4 percent), Vietnamese (4 percent), Japanese (1 percent), or some other language (3 percent).

Please indicate if the service is available to pollworkers through your office's hotline(s).			
	Available Through Hotline	Not Available but Hotline Refers Caller to Appropriate Person/ Office	Not Available and Hotline Does Not Refer Caller
	%	%	%
Election Day hotlines for poll workers (clarification on laws and procedures, troubleshooting with voting system problems, "no-show" poll workers, missing supplies, etc.)	71	27	3
Pre-Election Day hotlines for poll workers (clarifica-tion on laws and proce-dures, troubleshooting with voting system problems, etc.)	64	29	8
Poll worker recruiting and poll worker informa-tion (assignment, training schedule, etc.)	57	37	5
Automated system for poll workers to signal the open/ closed station of that polling location	25	30	44

When only jurisdictions that are required to publish election materials in a language other than English are considered, the prevalence of hotlines with foreign language assistance increases. Nearly two-thirds (65 percent) of jurisdictions that are required to publish materials in a language other than English report that their hotline offers support in a language other than English while 35 percent of these jurisdictions say their hotlines operate solely in English. By contrast, 15 percent of those jurisdictions that are not required to publish materials in a foreign language offer foreign language support through their hotline, but that a vast majority (85 percent) of them operate their hotline solely in English.

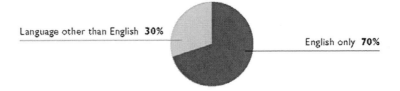

Does your office's hotline(s) operate solely in English or do you offer support in a language other than English?

Language other than English 30%

English only 70%

Nearly One-Half of Hotlines Have Some Form of TTY or TDD Technology Support for the Hearing Impaired

Roughly one-fourth (27 percent) of jurisdictions report that their hotline is directly equipped with telephone typewriter (TTY) or telecommunications device for the deaf (TTD) technology for the hearing impaired. An additional 19 percent of jurisdictions say they do not directly provide support in TTY or TDD technology but have a relay program with a State-level service.

Just over one-half of jurisdictions report that they do not offer any TTY or TDD support—either directly or through a relay program. Breaking these results down by the level of government of election office shows that 39 percent of States responding to the survey and 58 percent of county/city/township election offices do not offer TTY or TDD nor do they coordinate this support with another agency.

Is your hotline number(s) equipped with TTY or TDD technology for the hearing impaired?	
Yes, hotline directly TTY / TDD	27%
Yes, have relay program with a State-level service	19%
No, not offered and callers not relayed/transferred	55%

Most Calls to Hotlines are about Registration and Voting Location Issues

Jurisdictions with dedicated hotlines report that the bulk of the calls they receive have to do with issues with where to go to vote (42 percent) or about checking on registration status (33 percent). Jurisdictions report that fewer than 2 in 10 calls are about receipt of absentee ballots (8 percent), general nonfraud complaints (6 percent), or fraud-related concerns (1 percent).

Thinking only about the calls made to your hotline(s) on Election Day, approximately what percentage of calls are made to the following categories?	
Where do I vote?	42%
Am I registered?	33%
Did you get my absentee ballot?	8%
I have a complaint (nonfraud related)	6%
I suspect fraud	1%
Other	14%

These are self-reported percentages reported directly from jurisdictions and do not sum to 100 percent.

Few Jurisdictions Have Hotlines Answered Exclusively by Automated System

Fewer than one in five jurisdictions have hotlines that are answered exclusively by an automated system (17 percent). Instead, most jurisdictions report that a live operator answers their office's hotline (66 percent) or they have both a hotline answered by a live operator and one answered by an automated system (17 percent).

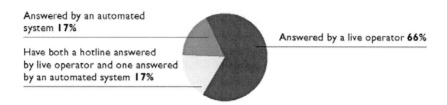

Are your information lines or hotlines answered by a live operator or are they answered by an automated system or do you have both kinds of hotlines?

- Answered by an automated system **17%**
- Have both a hotline answered by live operator and one answered by an automated system **17%**
- Answered by a live operator **66%**

Most Automated Systems Have the Ability to Speak to a Live Operator

Although few jurisdictions have hotlines answered exclusively by automated systems, the majority (76 percent) of those that do allow callers to opt out of the automated portion and speak to a live operator. Only one-fourth (24 percent) are completely automated systems.

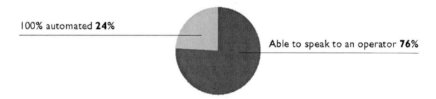

Are callers able to exit the automated portion of the phone information hotline and speak to an operator or is your hotline 100 percent automated?

- 100% automated **24%**
- Able to speak to an operator **76%**

Asked only of those who have a hotline answered by an automated system.

Operators Use a Variety of Sources to Handle Voters' Information Needs

Local-level jurisdictions that operate hotlines that are answered by a live operator use a variety of tools to answer voters' information needs. Nearly all local-level jurisdictions that have operator-answered hotlines give their operators access to voter registration (91 percent) or polling-place lookup databases (86 percent). A large majority also give their operators access to absentee ballot databases. Roughly one-half (49 percent) employ a poll worker management database to help operators handle questions that come into the hotline and 4 in 10 utilize a provisional ballot database (40 percent).

What is more, three-fourths (74 percent) of these jurisdictions say their operators have access to three or more of these databases and almost one-third (30 percent) give their operators access to all five data sources.

What databases, if any, do your hotline operators have access to?	
Voter registration database	91%
Polling-place lookup database	86%
Absentee ballot database	70%
Poll worker management database	49%
Provisional ballot database	40%

Asked only of local-level jurisdictions with hotlines answered by a live operator (n=43).

Among Automated Hotlines, Integration With Voter Registration and Polling- Place Lookup Databases are Most Common

What databases, if any, are integrated with your hotline(s) system(s)?	
Voter registration database	45%
Polling-place lookup database	33%
Absentee ballot database	10%
Poll worker management database	10%
Provisional ballot database	10%

Asked only of local-level jurisdictions with hotlines answered by a live operator (n=21).

Voter registration and polling-place lookup databases are the most popular databases for local-level jurisdictions with automated systems to integrate into their hotlines. Forty-five percent of local-level jurisdictions with automated hotline systems integrate voter registration databases and 33 percent integrate a polling-place lookup database. A small number report integrating an absentee ballot database (10 percent), poll worker management database (10 percent) or provisional ballot database (10 percent).

At the same time, database integration for those jurisdictions that have their hotlines answered by automated systems is not completely widespread. Roughly 4 in 10 jurisdictions with automated hotlines do not report any database integration and only 14 percent say they have three or more databases integrated directly into their automated hotline. Further conversations with these jurisdictions show that many jurisdictions in this category use the automated system to route calls to particular offices or operators, but the bulk of the voter information services are handled by live persons and not through database integration and, in this way, are similar to operator-answered hotlines in their information management and dissemination strategies.

State-Run Hotlines Use Information Gathered at the Local Level to Inform Voters

State-level election offices use a variety of tools to give information to citizens calling into their hotlines. The majority of States that responded to the survey say that their hotline has access to statewide voter registration lists (69 percent).

Does your hotline have access to statewide voter registration lists?

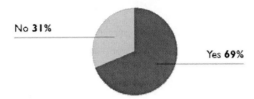

No 31% Yes 69%

Asked only of State-level jurisdictions.

In addition, most State-level hotlines have the ability to give voters the phone number of their local-level elections office. One-half (50 percent) of States have a database of phone numbers for local-level jurisdictions directly on the hotline operators' computer and an additional 25 percent have a hard-copy list of phone numbers available to reference. Only one-fourth of State-run hotlines do not have the ability to give voters the direct phone number of the appropriate local-level elections office.

States are equally split in their ability to give voters the phone number of voter information hotlines operated by local-level jurisdictions in their State. One-half (50 percent) report that they have a list of voter information hotlines operated by subordinate jurisdictions and one-half (50 percent) say they do not.

Is your office's hotline able to give callers the general contact information for their specific county/township election office?

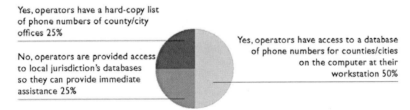

Yes, operators have a hard-copy list of phone numbers of county/city offices 25%

No, operators are provided access to local jurisdiction's databases so they can provide immediate assistance 25%

Yes, operators have access to a database of phone numbers for counties/cities on the computer at their workstation 50%

Asked only of State-level jurisdictions.

Does your office have a list of voter information hotlines operated by subordinate jurisdictions in your State?

Yes 50% No 50%

Asked only of State-level jurisdictions.

Most Operator-Answered Hotlines Lack a Systematic Approach to Dealing with Voters' Inquiries

A large majority (73 percent) of State and local-level jurisdictions with operator-answered hotlines say that they use a nonstructured and nonautomated approach to respond to callers' questions.

Of those who use a more systematic approach, protocol cards, forms, and checklist scripts are the most popularly used systems. Roughly one-fourth (23 percent) of responding jurisdictions report that they use protocol cards, forms, and/or checklist scripts. Two percent used an automated script or protocol software system and an additional 2 percent say they use both protocol cards and an automated software system.

Do your call-takers have a protocol card, form, checklist, and script or software system to guide their interaction with callers OR does your office use a nonstructured and nonautomated approach to respond to callers' questions?	
Use a nonstructured and nonautomated approach	73%
Use protocol cards/form/checklist script	24%
Use automated script/protocol software system	2%
Use BOTH protocol cards/form/checklist script and an automated software system	2%

Asked only of those with operator-answered only systems.

Few Hotlines Formally Track Information on Hotline Calls

Just fewer than one-half (45 percent) of automated hotline systems have the ability to track the wait time of calls and one-third (33 percent) can track call volume. Only 1 in 10 jurisdictions with an automated hotline system report that they have the ability to track the duration of a call (10 percent), the type of call (10 percent), or the end result of each call (10 percent).

Does your automated hotline system have the following features to track calls?	
Wait time of a call	45%
Call volume	33%
Disposition or end result of each call	10%
The type or category of a call	10%
Duration of a call	10%

Asked only of jurisdictions with automated hotline systems.

Do you currently track the type of call or information being sought after by the caller (for example, polling-place lookup or absentee ballot status)?

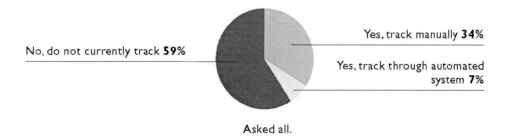

Asked all.

Similarly, the majority (59 percent) of jurisdictions, whether they have automated or operator-answered hotlines, do not currently track the type of calls or information being sought after by callers. One-third (34 percent) of jurisdictions have a manual system for tracking the type of calls, and an additional 7 percent track the type of calls, through their automated system.

(See Section Eight, Sampling of Best Practices, for Clark County, Nevada's "Line of Business" program, which tracks calls by type.)

Hotlines Quick to Answer Citizens' Calls

A majority of jurisdictions report that callers to their hotlines wait on average less than 1 minute. An additional 2 in 10 said that callers wait 1 to 2 (15 percent) or 2 to 3 (7 percent) minutes. Very few jurisdictions report wait times longer than 3 minutes or longer and almost 2 in 10 jurisdictions report that they did not have enough information to give estimates on wait times.

What is the average wait time for calls made to your hotline?

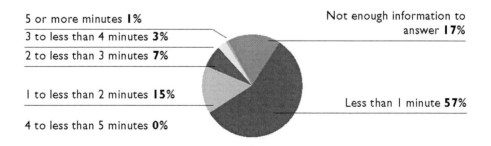

Most Calls Last Only a Minute or Two

What is the average duration of calls made to your hotline once a caller is connected (not including hold time)?	
5 or more minutes	1%
4 to less than 5 minutes	26%
3 to less than 4 minutes	7%
2 to less than 3 minutes	26%
1 to less than 2 minutes	38%
Less than 1 minute	8%
Not enough information to answer	15%

Jurisdictions with dedicated hotlines report that the bulk of calls received to their hotlines last only 1 to 2 (38 percent) or 2 to 3 (26 percent) minutes. Many fewer report that the average call is less than 1 minute (8 percent) or more than 3 minutes (12 percent).

Fifteen percent of jurisdictions report that they do not have enough information to estimate the average duration of calls.

Hotlines Typically Fall into Two Categories—High Volume and Low Volume

When it comes to call volume, hotlines tend to fit into two groups: those that receive only one or two calls at a time (25 percent) and those that handle a high volume of calls and are capable of receiving seven or more calls at one time (40 percent).

Closer inspection of the data shows that this bimodal distribution of call capability is driven mainly by those jurisdictions with hotlines answered by live operators. In the main, there appear to be two types of operator-answered hotlines- low-volume hotlines that answer only one to two calls at a time (30 percent) and hotlines capable of handling high call volumes and able to receive seven or more calls at a time (36 percent). However, the largest bulk (48 percent) of automated-answered hotlines fall into this latter category and are capable of receiving seven or more calls at a time.

Similarly, although almost one-half (46 percent) of the jurisdictions said that they did not have enough information about call volumes to estimate the largest number of calls received in one day, data from the jurisdictions that were able to make estimates show a similar grouping into low- and high-volume hotlines. Roughly as many jurisdictions received fewer than 100 calls on their highest volume day as received 5,000 or more calls.

Not surprisingly, automated hotlines and State-run hotlines tend to have higher call volumes than hotlines run by local-level jurisdictions and those answered by live operators. On the highest volume day, the median number of calls received by automated-answered hotlines was 6,000 calls and was 1,799 for State-run hotlines. By comparison, live operator-answered hotlines received a median of 200 calls on their highest volume day and the median number of calls reported from local-level jurisdictions is 350 calls on their highest volume day.

What is the number of incoming calls that can be received at one time?		
Automated Answered	1 to 2 calls	13%
	3 to 4 calls	0%
	5 to 6 calls	8%
	7 or more calls	48%
	Not enough information to answer	30%
Operator Answered	1 to 2 calls	30%
	3 to 4 calls	18%
	5 to 6 calls	14%
	7 or more calls	36%
	Not enough information to answer	2%

Historically, what is the largest number of calls received in one day?	
Fewer than 100 calls	11%
100 to 499	15%
500 to 999	3%
1,000 to 1,999	12%
2,000 to 2,999	3%
3,000 to 3,999	2%
4,000 to 4,999	3%
5,000 or more	12%
Not enough information to answer	46%

SECTION SIX: DEVELOPMENT OF HOTLINES

Nearly All Jurisdictions Say Developing a Hotline Was Easy

More than 8 in 10 jurisdictions with dedicated hotlines report that the process of developing the hotline was easy, with jurisdictions roughly equally split in whether they would describe the process as very (38 percent) or somewhat (45 percent) easy. Only a small minority of jurisdictions describe the process as somewhat (15 percent) or very (1 percent) hard.

Overall, how would you describe your office's experience developing the hotline?	
Very easy	38%
Somewhat easy	45%
Somewhat hard	15%
Very hard	1%

Jurisdictions with operator-answered hotlines find the process of developing the hotline a little bit easier than their counterparts who developed automated machine-answered hotlines. Roughly one-half (48 percent) of those operator- answered hotlines describe the development of their hotline as very easy compared with 17 percent of jurisdictions with automated machine-answered hotlines. Instead, the majority of these jurisdictions describe the process as somewhat easy (52 percent).

Majority of Hotlines are Developed in House

A two-thirds majority (68 percent) of jurisdictions report that they developed their dedicated hotline in house. About 2 in 10 jurisdictions chose to outsource some (9 percent) or most (13 percent) or the work, while 1 in 10 outsourced all of the development work for their hotline (9 percent).

Not surprising, given the level of technical skill required to develop an automated-answered hotline, hotlines answered by live operators were much more likely than their counterparts with automated-answered hotlines to have developed the hotline completely in house (82 percent vs. 40 percent) whereas jurisdictions that developed automated hotlines were more likely to outsource most or all of the work (10 percent vs. 48 percent). Jurisdictions with live operator and automated-answered hotlines were roughly equally likely to outsource some of the development work (8 percent vs. 12 percent).

Developing the hotline in house or outsourcing some or all of the development work does not have an impact on the ease of hotline development. Those who developed the hotline in house are as likely to describe the development of the hotline process as easy as those who outsourced the work in part or in whole.

Some jurisdictions stressed the importance of hiring a vendor with specific election experience, while others advised on the importance of hiring a firm with significant experience developing hotlines.

Did you develop the hotline in house or did you outsource most or all of the work to another company or organization?	
Developed the hotline in house	68%
Outsourced some of the development work	9%
Outsourced most of the development work	13%
Outsourced all of the development work	9%

All those Who Outsourced Work Indicated Satisfaction with Service Provider

All responding jurisdictions that outsourced at least some of the work report satisfaction with their service provider. In fact, 9 in 10 report high satisfaction with their service provider (91 percent) and the remaining jurisdictions say they were somewhat satisfied with their service provider (10 percent).

Most Hotlines Developed Relatively Quickly

A plurality (40 percent) of hotlines were developed from start to finish within 1 to 2 weeks, although 1 in 10 (10 percent) jurisdictions reports that it took them more than 2 months to develop their hotline.

There is only a very slight difference in the length of development between automated-answered and operator-answered hotlines. Thirty-one percent of automated-answered hotlines were developed in 1 to 2 weeks compared to 46 percent of live operator-answered hotlines. At the same time, jurisdictions with automated-answered hotlines were about as likely as jurisdictions with operator- answered hotlines to report taking more than 2 months in development (19 percent vs. 14 percent).

Approximately how many weeks did it take you to develop the hotline—from the time that you started planning the hotline features to when the hotline was fully operational?	
1 to 2 weeks	40%
3 to 4 weeks	15%
5 to 6 weeks	23%
7 to 8 weeks	13%
9 to 10 weeks	4%
More than 10 weeks	6%

How would you rate your satisfaction with this service provider?	
Very satisfied	91%
Somewhat satisfied	10%
Somewhat dissatisfied	0%
Very dissatisfied	0%

Hotline Development Does Not Have to be Costly

Nearly one-half (47 percent) of jurisdictions with dedicated hotlines opted not to answer questions about the cost of their hotline. However, based on the answers of the 41 jurisdictions that did provide costing information, we see that hotline development does not necessarily have to be an expensive affair. one-third (42 percent) report that they did not spend any money on developing their hotline and one-fourth (24 percent) spent less than $1,000 dollars. At the same time, a handful of jurisdictions spend $5,000 or more on developing and implementing their jurisdiction's hotline.

Follow on interviews with jurisdictions that indicated that the development of their hotline had cost very little revealed that most of them had benefited from having the hotline developed in house, which meant both by staff from the election department or from the city, county, or State technology information technology services or telecommunications departments. For example, the New York City Board of Elections had its Management Information Systems Department initiate a state-of-the-art Interactive Voice Response system in 2000. Another jurisdiction said, "We simply called the State Division of Information Services to have the number installed."

Perceptions of Customer Service Needs, More Than Costs, Drive the Decision about the Type of Hotline

More than three-fourths of jurisdictions with hotlines answered by an automated system say they chose this over a hotline answered by a live operator because of availability of staff (77 percent) or anticipated call volume (77 percent). Nearly as many say that calculations of wait times or time on hold (73 percent) and customer services needs (71 percent) drove their decision.

A majority say that the special needs of voters in their jurisdiction was part of their reasoning for choosing an automated hotline, but jurisdictions were split on whether special needs was a major (28 percent) or minor (33 percent) reason.

Similarly, jurisdictions are split in their evaluations of how important costs were to their decision making process. A majority say that cost was a reason for their choosing to have an automated hotline, but jurisdictions are split on whether costs were a major (33 percent) or minor (24 percent) consideration and a large number of jurisdictions (43 percent) say that costs were not a reason at all.

Why did your office choose to have an automated hotline rather than one answered by a live operator?			
	Major Reason	**Minor Reason**	**Not a Reason**
	%	%	%
Customer service	71	14	14
Costs	33	24	43
Availability of staff	77	14	9
Anticipated call volume	77	9	14
Wait times/time on hold	73	14	14
Special needs of voters in jurisdiction	28	33	39

Jurisdictions that opted for a live operator-answered hotline also cite customer service as major reason. In fact, for those with live operator-answered hotlines, customer service considerations far outstrip other considerations in informing their choice. One jurisdiction advised, "Always answer calls with a live operator. I apply this rule year round to all calls made to the Board of Elections but especially on Election Day when citizens are trying to determine whether or not and where to vote; I feel a live operator offers the most positive encouragement toward that end."

Why did your office choose to have a live operator-answered hotline rather than an automated one?			
	Major Reason	**Minor Reason**	**Not a Reason**
	%	%	%
Customer service	80%	8%	12%
Costs	20%	18%	61%
Availability of staff	29%	29%	43%
Anticipated call volume	39%	16%	45%
Wait times/time on hold	35%	20%	44%
Special needs of voters in jurisdiction	20%	41%	39%

Eight percent of jurisdictions say customer service was a major factor in their decision. Anticipated call volume (39 percent), wait times (35 percent), availability of staff (29 percent), and the special needs of voters (20 percent) were major reasons for choosing to have a live operator-answered hotline for many fewer jurisdictions.

Interestingly, a majority (61 percent) say that costs were not a reason for choosing to have a live operator-answered hotline over an automated one, although 20 percent of jurisdictions say costs were a major reason and 18 percent say costs were a minor reason.

Some jurisdictions indicated in followup interviews that voters do not like to deal with an automated line or phone tree, and they felt that a live operator was a better level of customer service. Other jurisdictions pointed out that since the majority of calls are to confirm registration and to ask the voting location, which can be easily provided via the automated functions, the automated capacity allowed them to reserve their live operators for questions that required customized interaction. In addition, automated lines allow voters to be provided service during nonoffice hours.

Still other jurisdictions have a blended approach- voters are advised that there will be a wait for a live operator, while the caller waits, he or she listens to prompts to access automated information or is referred to the jurisdiction's Web site.

SECTION SEVEN: MAINTENANCE AND OPERATION OF HOTLINES

Customer service-oriented and well-trained staff can be the key to a successful voter hotline. This means that a jurisdiction must recruit and track performance of staff, provide periodic training to staff, and provide staff with materials needed to respond accurately to voters.

Maintenance of Information Handled in House

Nearly all jurisdictions that operated dedicated hotlines during the 2006 election season handled all of the maintenance of the information for the hotline completely in house. Only 1 in 10 (10 percent) jurisdictions say they outsourced some of the maintenance work and no jurisdictions reported that they outsourced most or all of the day-to-day maintenance of information or databases used by their hotline. The few jurisdictions that did outsource this work report being satisfied with their service provider.

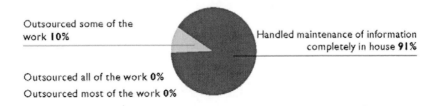

During election season, how often are updates made?	
In real time/as changes are made	68%
Daily	13%
Weekly	6%
Monthly	1%
Only at the end of the canvass/audit period	3%
None of the above	10%

During election season, three-fourths of jurisdictions make changes to the information accessed by hotline automated systems or operators on a daily basis. An additional more than 1 in 10 (13 percent) make daily updates, while a handful of jurisdictions make weekly (6 percent) or monthly (1 percent) updates.

When it comes to costs of database maintenance, only about 30 jurisdictions participating in the survey reported how much they spend. Of these, 29 percent say they incur no extra costs for updating the information for their phone hotline, although the median amount spent in 2006 was $500, and a few jurisdictions report having spent $1,000 or more on administration and personnel costs maintaining and/or updating the information for their dedicated phone hotline. Only one jurisdiction reported paying a per record fee for database maintenance.

Staffing of Hotlines also Handled In-House

Similar to the situation with the development of hotlines, few jurisdictions outsource a portion of the operations and staffing of their hotlines and no jurisdictions report outsourcing all of the day-to-day operation and staffing. Instead, nearly all (92 percent) jurisdictions handle the day-to-day operation and staffing completely in house.

The few jurisdictions that do outsource the operation and staffing of their hotline report being very satisfied with their service provider.

Does your office handle in house the day-to-day operation and staffing of the operators who take hotline calls or do you outsource some, most, or all of the staffing of the hotline staff to another company or organization?

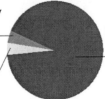

Outsourced some of the day-to-day operation and staffing **4%**

Outsourced most of the day-to-day operation and staffing **4%**

Outsourced all of the day-to-day operation and staffing **0%**

Handled day-to-day operation and staffing completely in house **92%**

During nonpeak times or seasons what is the average number of full-time and part-time hotline operators?			
	1st Quartile	Median	3rd Quartile
Full-time staff	1	2	6
Part-time staff	0	0	1

Asked only of jurisdictions with hotlines in which callers can talk to an operator.

During peak times or seasons what is the average number of full-time and part-time hotline operators?			
	1st Quartile	Median	3rd Quartile
Full-time staff	2	4	7
Part-time staff	1	2	7

Asked only of jurisdictions with hotlines in which callers can talk to an operator.

When operator-answered hotlines or automated-answered hotlines with the option of speaking to a live operator are in their busy season, they are typically staffed by about four full-time staff and two part-time staff, although this number typically ranges from two to seven full time staff and one to seven full-time staff.

During off-peak times or seasons, hotline staffing drops down to a median staffing arrangement of two full-time staff and no part-time staff with typical ranges falling between two to six full-time staff and no or only one part-time staff.

Shadowing is Most Popular Method of Training Operators

Shadowing of an experienced operator is the most popular method by which hotline operators are trained. Just over three-fourths of jurisdictions report that they use this method to train their hotline operators. Classroom lectures (43 percent) or role playing (41 percent) is employed by a sizable minority of jurisdictions while few (20 percent) jurisdictions use computer-based tutorials to train their hotline operators.

For each of the following, please indicate whether or not this method is used to train hotline operators.			
	Used	Not Used	Not Sure/Not Enough Information To Answer
	%	%	%
Classroom lectures	43	50	4
Role playing/simulated calls	41	50	7
Computer-based tutorial	20	67	7
Shadowing experienced operator or person	78	22	4

Asked only of jurisdictions with hotlines in which callers can talk to an operator.

Are all operators, regardless of their level of experience, trained before each major election cycle?

No 18% Yes 82%

Most Train All Operators for Each Major Election Cycle

Most (82 percent) reporting jurisdictions state that they train all operators before each major election cycle regardless of the operator's level of experience. By contrast, nearly one in five jurisdictions do not train or retrain all operators.

Oregon Secretary of State's Office

The Oregon Secretary of State's (SOS's) office has developed a training manual called "Election Questions and Answers," which is used to train call center representatives. The manual is an interactive tool that is "question-driven". There are links throughout the manual that anticipate followup questions that callers may have and/or provide additional details for call representatives to share with the caller.

Each call representative has the electronic manual on his or her computer desktop, and it is updated regularly. The manual allows the call reps to fulfill approximately 80 percent of the calls to the toll-free line. In addition, each call representative has speed-dial capability to every county election office as well as to the SOS office, so he or she can transfer callers as necessary when unable to fulfill the call.

One other application we developed for the call center is a GIS application that allows the call reps to provide callers with the physical location and hours of operation of every official ballot drop site in the State. Because Oregon is an all "vote by mail" State, the call center receives thousands of calls in the last 3 days from voters wanting to know where the nearest ballot drop site is located.

Performance of Operators Evaluated Mainly by Tracking Complaints

Jurisdictions with hotlines staffed by operators (61 percent) mainly track complaints to monitor the hotline for accuracy and security (61 percent) while 35 percent of jurisdictions periodically listen in on calls. One-fourth of jurisdictions (25 percent) report employing both methods.

Majority of Jurisdictions Verify Identity of Caller's Identity

A 6 in 10 majority (58 percent) of jurisdictions report verifying a hotline caller's identity, such as verifying the caller's Social Security number or date of birth. An additional 16 percent verify identity some of the time or in some instances (such as before giving the caller personal information). By contrast, one-fourth (26 percent) of jurisdictions say they do not check the caller's identity.

What, if any, systematic effort does your office undertake to monitor the hotline for accuracy, security, or other critical performance variables?			
	Used	Not Used	Not Sure/Not Enough Information To Answer
	%	%	%
Periodic listening in on calls	35	46	20
Tracking of complaints	61	26	11

Asked only of jurisdictions with hotlines in which callers can talk to an operator.

When a voter calls the hotline seeking information such as voting location, absentee ballot request, change of address, do you have a standardized procedure for verifying the caller's identity, such as verifying Social Security number or date of birth?

No 26%
Yes, sometimes 16%
Yes, always 58%

Many Jurisdictions Require Operators to Use a Password to Access Data

Although fewer than one-half of jurisdictions say that the data utilized by the hotline is secured behind a firewall, most jurisdictions that have hotlines that utilize operators require operators to use a password in order to secure data.

Which, if any, of the following security measures do you employ?			
	Yes	No	Not Sure/Not Enough Information To Answer
	%	%	%
The data utilized by the hotline(s) is secured behind a firewall	43	50	4
Operators need a secure password to access data*	80	3	17

Asked only of jurisdictions with hotlines in which callers can talk to an operator.

Jurisdictions Use Multi Pronged Approach to Publicize Hotlines

The most widely used method of publicizing phone hotlines by jurisdiction is placing the hotline number on the jurisdictions Web site. This is something that nearly 9 in 10 (87 percent) jurisdictions report doing. Roughly two-thirds or more of jurisdictions also have

90 U.S. Election Assistance Commission

posters or flyers available at polling places (74 percent), advertise the hotline number in election mailings, (71 percent) or place ads in local papers (65 percent). Many fewer employ outreach partners to get out the word on their hotline (43 percent) or list the number with the phone company operator (28 percent).

What methods, if any, do you use to inform voters about your voter hotline?	
Publicize number on office's or jurisdiction's Web site	87%
Handouts or posters at polling place	74%
Advertise number in election mailing/sample ballot	71%
Ads in local or community paper	65%
Advertise through outreach partners	43%
Phone company operator	28%

SECTION EIGHT: SAMPLING OF TIPS AND SUCCESSFUL PRACTICES

Implementation and Management Tips

Survey respondents provided the following advice for jurisdictions seeking to develop and/or enhance their phone systems:

- Make sure that the person who answers the hotline has access to the latest updated information.
- Have all the details and requirements mapped out before starting any programming. Remember to seek input from the line staff that answer and handle the calls.
- If you are going to supplement your phone team during peak seasons, bring the temporaries in early to assure a good-quality training program.
- Stress-test the lines prior to Election Day and install a backup generator to maintain the telephone computer bank in the event of loss of power.
- For the poll worker phone bank, anticipate every possible problem by talking with poll workers and thinking through the best ways to assist the caller.

Successful Practices: Hotlines

- **Clark County, Nevada.** Clark County, Nevada's "Line of Business" (LOB) program is an innovative way to track the types of calls coming in to an operator. When a call comes in, operators simply push an "LOB" button on their phone and then key in a three-digit code (see Appendix A), which allows the system to track type of call, length of call, etc.
- **New York City Board of Elections/"Vote NYC."** The Board of Elections operates an attended phone bank supporting up to 80 simultaneous users during office hours (Monday–Friday, 9 a.m.–5 p.m.) with a multilingual staff of operators speaking English, Chinese Mandarin/Cantonese, Korean, and Spanish. (Toll free: 1-866-Vote-NYC.)

Callers using the phone bank can obtain information on poll sites (location, accessibility status, candidate list, interpretation), registration deadlines, voter status, names and addresses of elected officials, election data, candidates and ballots, voting machine write-ins and requests for Campaign Finance Board Voter Guides.

In 2000 the Board, through its Management Information Systems Department, initiated a state-of-the-art Interactive Voice Response (IVR) system. The use of the 24-hour, 7-days-a-week IVR system freed up staff to assist other callers. It also enabled callers after office hours to still receive the services or information that was needed. The IVR system features multlanguage recordings in English, Spanish, Chinese/Cantonese, and Korean; allows callers to request forms or flyers to be delivered direct via fax; and provides a voice recorder for callers to request voter registration forms and absentee ballot applications and other special requests. Calls received after business hours are returned by an operator on the following business day.

New York City also has a program in which voters can call 311 (similar to 411) and get election information.

- Maricopa County, Arizona. The Maricopa County Election Office historically tracked election hotline phone calls by completing call slips, which were at some point distributed to the appropriate department for action. In 2006, the office created an online database, which is available to anyone in the office to input data from hotline calls relating to the election. The central database serves as an information distribution center, allowing for rapid input from multiple locations, instant notification for timely resolution, summary analysis with numerous sorting and reporting abilities—plus all of this information is available to the entire office staff at any time. By developing this central database, the staff can quickly identify the quantity of calls that are received and what type of calls are being processed. For example, if large quantities of calls are received on new equipment or polling place procedures, the staff would note that adjustments need to be made to training of poll workers prior to the next election. This tool also provides quantifiable documentation to support proposals in election legislation, respond to media reports, and reinforce administrative decisions.

- Indiana. The offices of the Attorney General and Secretary of State in Indiana want to make it easy for voters to report fraud or other criminal activity on Election Day. Any voter can call a toll-free number to report any suspicious activity, such as ballot tampering and voters voting in the wrong precinct.

"This should send a clear message—we're serious about vote fraud and making sure each legitimate vote counts," Secretary of State Todd Rokita said.

Lake County, Indiana, however, is the only county in Indiana to implement its own toll-free hotline. The Indiana State vote fraud hotline is paid for with Federal funds and is monitored by the State's Joint Vote Fraud Task Force.

C. Successful Practices: Phone Banks Supplements/Alternatives

Offering information via Web site as an alternative to phone banks.

- **New York State.** In the fall of 2007, New York State joined other election offices nationwide to offer citizens the ability to access the voter registration database on line to verify their registration.

"Many people ask county boards and us if they're registered. They forget … this will just make it easier," said Lee Daghlian, New York State Board of Elections

- **Colorado.** Local election officials continue to look to the Web as an opportunity to put voter information at the fingertips of voters in their jurisdiction. In Jefferson County, Colorado, a new feature was launched in 2007 that allows voters to track the status of their ballot. By entering their name and date of birth, voters can look up their voter information and also view the date that their ballot was mailed, the date it was returned, and the date it was processed.

"It is our hope that this new feature allowing voters to check the status of their ballots will increase voter participation and confidence in the election process," said County Clerk & Recorder Pam Anderson.

- **Federal Voting Assistance Program (FVAP).** States and territories are making it easier to determine voter registration status. Twenty-two states, Puerto Rico, and the District of Columbia have Web sites where voters can check their registration status. The FVAP has compiled a list of jurisdictions that provide important voter services, such as voter registration status checks, status of provisional ballots, and online sample ballots (www.fvap.gov/vao/stregissites.html). The large number of jurisdictions who are moving their business to the Web clearly shows the nationwide trend of the Web being used as a portal for voters on key election information.
- **Johnson County, Kansas.** The Johnson County, Kansas, election office launched its Web site in January 1996 and immediately offered voters the ability to find their polling place. Since then, additional online services have been provided, including the ability to verify voter registration status and view/print a sample ballot. Other online services provided in the last few years include an online poll worker training module.

Johnson County Election Office

Election Commissioner
Connie Schmidt

connie.schmidt@jocoks.com

★ Back to Election Office Home Page

Information is updated nightly between 2:00 a.m. and 4:00 a.m.

Sample Ballots are posted no later than 20 days prior to Election Day.

To help us locate your voter registration record, please enter your information and then click the [Look Me Up] button.

Register to Vote

Find Voter Record

First Name :	Last Name :		Date Of Birth :
		AND	
			Ex: MM/DD/YYYY

Look Me Up

Polling Place Summary

Poll Location :

WHEATRIDGE MIDDLE SCHOOL

Poll Address :

318 E WASHINGTON ST

GARDNER, KS 66030

Voter Instructions :

LOBBY. DISABLED ENTRANCE: MAIN ENTRANCE.

Show Map

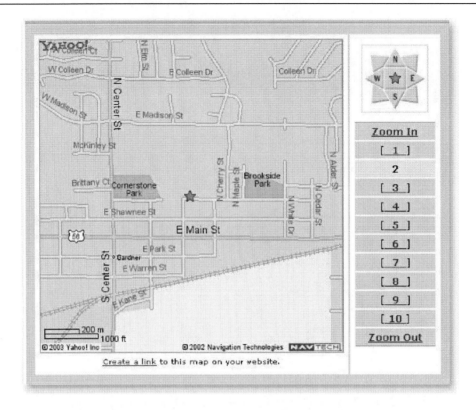

Text messaging and podcasting are the next generation of communication tools to be offered to voters. Beginning in 2005, under the leadership of Election

Commissioner Brian Newby, the Johnson County, Kansas election office provides voters the opportunity to sign up and receive important election updates and alerts on their cell phone, wireless PDA pager and/or e-mail. Examples of information provided through this service include: announcements of upcoming elections, early voting dates and locations, reminders prior to Election Day, and other urgent information such as last-minute polling place changes. Visit www. jocoelection.org for examples of how this new communication is managed.

APPENDIX A. CLARK COUNTY'S "LINE OF BUSINESS" (LOB) CODES (CODES FOR TRACKING INCOMING CALLS BY TYPE)

Daily Codes
- 001 Registration Misc. Questions
- 002 Voter verifying his Reg. Info
- 003 Verifying another's Reg. Info
- 004 What is my prec./polling place?
- 005 Who are my Representatives?
- 006 Voter needs an Application
- 007 Voter needs a Reg. Card

| 008 | Complaints about Spanish |
| 009 | Administration Calls |

Mail Ballot Codes
010	Mail Ballot Misc. Questions
011	Request for a Mail Ballot
012	Voter did not receive Ballot
013	Needs Mail Ballot Instructions
014	When do I return my Ballot?
015	Can I vote at the Polls instead?
016	Did you receive my Mail Ballot?
017	I spoiled my Mail Ballot

Candidate Filing Codes
020	Candidate Filing Misc. Questions
021	Voter requests info. on candidates
022	Candidate Report questions
023	When is candidate filing period?

Sample Ballot Codes
030	Misc. Sample Ballot questions
031	Received wrong sample ballot
032	Did not get sample ballot
033	Lost sample ballot
034	Person does not live there

Early Voting Codes
040	Early Voting Misc. Questions
041	Requesting Early Voting Info.
042	Complaints about EV process
043	EV Personnel complaints
044	EV facility complaints
045	Wants EV turnout Figures
046	Likes Early Voting

Specific LOB Codes

Voteline Codes
050	Voteline Misc. Questions
051	Where is my Polling Place?
052	What are the Poll hours?
053	Husband/wife in Diff. Precincts
054	Need a ride to the polls
055	I want to change my party
056	Am I registered to vote?

057   Polling Place complaints

Team Leader Codes

060   Team leader Misc. Questions
061   Voter's name not on roster
062   Voter's party incorrect
063   Voter's name mis-spelled
064   No signature in Roster
065   Roster says already voted
066   Voter is inactive
067   Voter is cancelled
068   Roster says ID required
069   Citizenship questioned
070   Voter Challenged

APPENDIX B. U.S. ELECTION ASSISTANCE COMMISSION VOTER HOTLINE SURVEY

BACKGROUND

The U.S. Election Assistance Commission has commissioned The Pollworker Institute (PI) and the International Foundation for Election Systems (IFES) to conduct a survey on phone-based information lines. The data will serve as the basis for a report to the EAC that highlights the experiences and opinions of people like you who set-up, operate, and maintain the country's voter and pollworker phone hotlines.

This survey is for research purposes only. We are not selling anything nor are we are associated with any political party or candidate. Your participation is voluntary and all of your answers will be kept strictly confidential and will not be connected to your name or the name of your office.

This survey should be completed by the person in your office most knowledgeable about your office's phone hotlines and/or voter information programs. If there is someone in your office who is more knowledgeable, please give your log-on and password to the person and request that he or she complete the survey.

No matter how small or big your offices' phone-based information services are it is still important that you complete the survey help us collect the most scientifically valid results possible.

Q1. Please indicate your level of government:
1.   Federal [GO TO Q4a]
2.   State [GO TO Q3b]
3.   County [GO TO Q2a]
4.   City [GO TO Q2b]
9.   (No answer) [GO TO Q3a]

Voter Information Websites Study

IF COUNTY OFFICE, ASK:

Q2a.What county or counties does your office serve?

    [Open text response] [GO TO Q3a]

    9 (No answer)

IF CITY OFFICE, ASK:

Q2b.What town/city does your office serve?

    [Open text response] [GO TO Q3a]

    9 (No answer)

IF COUNTY OR CITY OFFICE, ASK:

Q3a. And what state is this jurisdiction in?

    [Dropdown menu with list of states] [GO TO Q4a]

    9 (No answer)

IF STATE OFFICE, ASK:

Q3b. What state does your office serve?

    [Dropdown menu with list of states] [GO TO Q4a]

    9 (No answer)

Q4a.During the 2006 Election season, did your office operate a phone-based information line, phone b or "hotline" to provide services or information to voters or pollworkers in your area?

    1. Yes [GO TO 4b]

    2. No [GO TO Q52]

    9. (No answer) [GO TO 4b]

Q4b. And was this information line or "hotline" the same as your office's main number or did you have a phone number dedicated specifically to providing information to voters and/or pollworkers?

    1. Same as office main number [GO TO 4c]

    2. Dedicated phone number [GO TO Q5]

    9. (No answer) [GO TO Q4c]

Q4c. How does your office handle provisional ballots?

    [Open text response] [GO TO Q52]

    9 (No answer) [GO TO Q52]

IF HOTLINE, ASK:

Q5. How many dedicated phone information lines or "hotlines" did your office operate?

    __ __ Record 2-digit response]

    9999 (No answer)

IF ONLY ONE HOTLINE, ASK:

Q6a.Was this information hotline toll-free (1-800) or a normal toll-call hotline?

    1. Voter hotline toll-free (1-800) [GO TO Q7]

2. Normal toll-call hotline [GO TO Q7]
9. (No answer) [GO TO Q7]

IF MORE THAN ONE HOTLINE, ASK:
Q6b. Please indicate how many, if any, of these hotlines are toll-free (1-800) and how many are normal call phone numbers.

___ ___ toll-free (1-800)
___ ___ normal toll-call
9999 (No answer)

Q7. For each of the following, please indicate when, if at all, your information line(s) or "hotline(s)" are operation
A   On Election Day
   1. None, not in operation
   2. All day / 24 hours
   3. During normal office hours
   4. Other (specify) _____
B   During election season (excluding Election Day)
   1. None, not in operation
   2. 24 hours / 7-days a week
   3. During normal office hours
   4. Other (specify) _____
C   The remainder of the year, outside of the main election season
   1. None, not in operation
   2. 24 hours / 7-days a week
   3. During normal office hours
   4. Other (specify)_____

Q8. For each of the following areas of election services, please indicate if the service is available to voters through any of your office's toll-free phone hotline(s), normal toll-call hotline(s), or not offered. (multiple responses accepted)

	Yes, available through toll-free hotline	Yes, available through normal toll hotline	No, but caller is referred to appropriate person / office	Not available and caller not referred	(No answer)
Voter registration – am I registered?	1	2	3	4	9
Request or check status of absentee ballot	1	2	3	4	9
Information on legal deadlines to request/ return absentee ballot	1	2	3	4	9
Information on voting location and hours	1	2	3	4	9

Voter Information Websites Study

(Continued)

	Yes, available through toll-free hotline	Yes, available through normal toll hotline	No, but caller is referred to appropriate person / office	Not available and caller not referred	(No answer)
Information on voting system used in voter's polling place	1	2	3	4	9
Information on accessibility provisions in polling locations for voters with disabilities	1	2	3	4	9
Provisional ballot status	1	2	3	4	9
Voter information specific to Overseas and Military Voters (UOCAVA ballot sent, received (status))	1	2	3	4	9
How to be a pollworker	1	2	3	4	9
Clarification of laws and/or procedures	1	2	3	4	9
Report fraud – file HAVA complaint	1	2	3	4	9
Other general voter complaints/concerns	1	2	3	4	9

Q9. Please indicate if this is available to *pollworkers* through your office's toll-free phone hotline(s), normal toll-call hotline, or not offered.

	Yes, available through toll-free hotline	Yes, available through normal toll hotline	Not offered	(No answer)
Pollworker recruiting and pollworker information (assignment, training schedule, etc.)	1	2	3	9
Election Day Hotlines for Pollworkers (clarification on laws and procedures, troubleshooting with voting system problems, "no-show" pollworkers, missing supplies, etc.)	1	2	3	9
Pre- Election Day Hotlines for Pollworkers (clarification on laws and procedures, troubleshooting with voting system problems, etc.)	1	2	3	9
Automated system for pollworkers to signal the open/closed station of that polling location	1	2	3	9

Q10. Thinking *only* about the calls made to your hotline(s) on Election Day, approximately what percent of calls are made to the following categories? (Just your best guess is fine)

_ _ _ % Am I registered?
_ _ _ % Where do I vote?
_ _ _ % Did you get my absentee ballot?
_ _ _ % I suspect fraud
_ _ _ % I have a complaint (non-fraud related)
_ _ _ % Other (specify) _____
9999 (No answer)

Q11. Does your office's hotline(s) operate solely in English or do you offer support in a language other t English?
1. English only
2. Languages other than English
9. (No answer)

IF LANGUAGE OTHER THAN ENGLISH AVAILABLE, ASK:
Q12. Which, if any, of the following languages are available (directly or via a referral program) through y office's hotline(s)?

	Available	**Not available**	**(No answer)**
Chinese	1	2	9
Japanese	1	2	9
Korean	1	2	9
Spanish	1	2	9
Tagalog	1	2	9
Vietnamese	1	2	9
Other language(s) (specify)	1	2	9

Q13. Is your hotline number(s) equipped with TTY or TTD technology for the hearing impaired?
1. Yes, hotline directly TTY / TTD
2. Yes, have relay program with a state-level service
3 No, not offered and callers not relayed/transferred
9. (No answer)

IF ONLY ONE HOTLINE, ASK:
Q14a. Is your information line or hotline initially answered by a live operator (even if momentarily put on hold) or is it answered by an automated system?
1. Answered by a live operator
2. Answered by an automated system
9. (No answer)

IF MORE THAN ONE HOTLINE, ASK:

Voter Information Websites Study

Q14b. Are your information lines or hotlines answered by a live operator or are they answered by an automated system or do you have both kinds of hotlines?

1. Answered by a live operator
2. Answered by an automated system
3. Have both a hotline answered by live operator and one answered by automated system
9. (No answer)

IF HAVE HOTLINE ANSWERED BY A LIVE OPERATOR, ASK:

Q15a. Why did your office choose to have a live-operator hotline rather than an automated one? For each of the following, please indicate whether this was a "minor reason", "major reason", or "not a reason".

	Minor reason	Major reason	Not a reason	(No answer)
A. Customer service				
B.Costs	1	2	3	9
C. Availability of staff	1	2	3	9
D. Anticipated call volume	1	2	3	9
E. Wait times / time on hold	1	2	3	9
F. Special needs of voters in jurisdiction	1	2	3	9
G. Other (specify_____)	1	2	3	9

IF HAVE AUTOMATED HOTLINE, ASK:

Q15b. Why did your office choose to have an automated hotline rather than one answered by a live operator? For each of the following, please indicate whether this was a "minor reason", "major reason", or "not a reason."

	Minor reason	Major reason	Not a reason	(No answer)
A.Customer service	1	2	3	9
B. Costs				
C. Availability of staff	1	2	3	9
D. Anticipated call volume	1	2	3	9
E. Wait times / time on hold	1	2	3	9
F. Special needs of voters in jurisdiction	1	2	3	9
G. Other (specify_____)	1	2	3	9

For the next few questions, please think back to when you *first developed* your office's information line or hotline to provide service or information to voters and/or pollworkers. (If your office operates more than one hotline, please think about the most recent hotline developed by your office).

U.S. Election Assistance Commission

Q16. Overall, how would you describe your office's experience developing the hotline? Would you say the overall process for developing the hotline was very easy, somewhat easy, somewhat hard or very hard?
1. Very easy
2. Somewhat easy
3. Somewhat hard
4. Very hard
9. (No answer)

Q17. And did you develop the hotline in-house or did you outsource most or all of the work to another company or organization?
1. Developed the hotline in-house
2. Outsourced some of the development work
3. Outsourced most of the development work
4. Outsourced all of the development work
9. (No answer)

IF OUTSOURCE SOME, MOST, OR ALL, ASK:
Q18. How would you rate your satisfaction with this service provider?
1. Very satisfied
2. Somewhat satisfied
3. Somewhat unsatisfied
4. Very unsatisfied
9. (No answer)

Q19. Approximately how many weeks did it take you to develop the hotline—from the time that you started planning the hotlines features to when the hotline was fully operational?
___ ___ weeks
9999 (No answer)

Q20. Approximately, how much did it cost for your office to develop and implement the hotline?
___ ___ USD
9999 (No answer)

Q21. What advice would you offer to another jurisdiction like yours that is planning to develop its own hotline to provide services and/or information to voters or pollworkers?
[open-ended text box]
9 (No answer)

IF HAVE AUTOMATED HOTLINE: For the next several questions, we'd like you to think about the *gathering and maintenance of the information* used by your phone information hotline (If your office operates more than one hotline, please think about the most recent hotline developed by your office).

IF HAVE OPERATOR-ANSWERED HOTLINE: For the next several questions, we'd like you to think about the *day-to-day operation of your* phone information hotline (If your office operates more than one hotline, please think about the most recent hotline developed by your office).

Q22. Does your office handle in-house the day-to-day maintenance of information and/or databases used by your hotline or do you outsource some, most or all of the work to another company or organization?
1. Handle maintenance of information completely in-house
2. Outsourced some of the work
3. Outsourced most of the work
4. Outsourced all of the work
9. (No answer)

IF OUTSOURCE SOME, MOST, OR ALL, ASK:
Q23. How would you rate your satisfaction with this service provider?
1. Very satisfied
2. Somewhat satisfied
3. Somewhat unsatisfied
4. Very unsatisfied
9. (No answer)

IF HAVE OPERATOR-ANSWERED HOTLINE, ASK:
Q24. Do your call-takers have a protocol card, form, checklist script or software system to guide their interaction with callers OR does your office use a non-structured and non-automated approach to respond to callers questions?
1. Use protocol cards/form /checklist script
2. Use automated script/protocol software system
3. Use BOTH protocol cards/form/checklist script and an automated software system
4. Use a non-structured and non-automated approach
9. (No answer)

IF HAVE OPERATOR-ANSWERED HOTLINE, ASK:
Q25a. What databases, if any, do your hotline operators have access to?
1. Voter registration database
2. Pollworker management database
3. Absentee ballot database
4. Provisional ballot database
5. Polling-place lookup database
9. (No answer)

IF ONE AUTOMATED HOTLINE, ASK:

Q25b. What databases, if any, are integrated with your hotline(s) system?
1. Voter registration database
2. Pollworker management database
3. Absentee ballot database
4. Provisional ballot database
5. Polling-place lookup database
9. (No answer)

IF MORE THAN AUTOMATED ONE HOLTILNE, ASK:
Q25c. Thinking about all the hotlines your office operates to provide information or services to voters or pollworkers, what databases, if any, are integrated with your hotline(s) system?
1. Voter registration database
2. Pollworker management database
3. Absentee ballot database
4. Provisional ballot database
5. Polling-place lookup database
9. (No answer)

IF STATE OFFICE, ASK:
Q26. Does your hotline have access to statewide voter registration lists?
1. Yes
2. No
9. (No answer)

IF STATE OFFICE, ASK:
Q27. Is your office's hotline able to give callers the general contact information for their specific county/township election office?
1. Yes, operators have a hard copy list of phone numbers of county/city offices.
2. Yes, operators have access to a database of phone numbers for counties/cities on the computer at their workstation.
3. Operators are provided access to local jurisdiction's databases so they can provide immediate assistance.
9. (No answer)

IF STATE OFFICE, ASK:
Q28. Does your office have a list of voter information hotlines operated by subordinate jurisdictions in your state?
1. Yes
2. No
9. (No answer)

IF HAVE AUTOMATED SYSTEM, ASK:
Q29a. During election season, how often are updates made to the system?
1. In real time / as changes are made
2. Daily

3. Weekly
4. Monthly
5. Only at the end of the canvass/audit period
6. None of the above
9. (No answer)

IF HAVE OPERATOR-ANSWERED HOTLINE, ASK:

Q29b. During election season, how often are updates made to the information operators have access to?
1. In real time/as changes are made
2. Daily
3. Weekly
3. Monthly
4. Only at the end of the canvass/audit period
5. None of the above
9. (No answer)

Q30. Over the last year, what where the total costs including administration and personnel costs associated with maintaining and/or updating the information for your phone hotline?
___ ___ USD
9999 (No answer)

ONLY IF HAVE AUTOMATED HOTLINE, ASK:

Q31. Is there a database maintenance charge per record?
1. Yes
2. No
9. (No answer)

IF CHARGE, ASK:

Q32. What is the monetary charge per call?
___ ___ USD
9999 (No answer)

IF AUTOMATED HOTLINE, ASK:

Q33a. What advice about information gathering and maintenance would you offer to a jurisdiction such as yours that is setting up a voter hotline?
[open-ended text box]
9 (No answer)

IF OPERATOR-ANSWERED HOTLINE, ASK:

Q33b. What advice about the day-to-day operation of a hotline would you offer to a jurisdiction such as yours that is setting up a voter hotline?
[open-ended text box]
9 (No answer)

IF AUTOMATED HOTLINE, ASK:

Q34. Does your automated hotline system have the following features to track the....

	Yes	No	(No answer)
wait time of calls	1	2	9
duration of calls	1	2	9
the type or category of call			
disposition or end result of each call	1	2	9
call volume			

Q35. Do you currently track the type of call or information being sought after by the caller (for example, polling place lookup or absentee ballot status, etc.)?
1. Yes, track manually
2. Yes, track through automated system
3. No, don't currently track
9 (No answer)

Q36. What is the average wait time for calls made to your hotline? (just your best guess is fine)

___ ___

98 not enough information to answer
99 (no answer)

Q37. What is the average duration of calls made to your hotline once a caller is connected (not including hold time)? (just your best guess is fine)

___ ___

98 not enough information to answer
99 (no answer)

Q38. What is the number of incoming calls that can be received at one time?

___ ___ ___ ___

98 not enough information to answer
99 (no answer)

Q39. Historically, what is the largest number of calls received in one day?

___ ___ ___ ___

98 not enough information to answer
99 (no answer)

IF AUTOMATED HOTLINE, ASK:
Q40. Are callers able to exit the automated portion of the phone information hotline and speak to an operator or is your hotline 100% automated?
1. able to speak to an operator
2. 100% automated
9. (No answer)

ONLY IF ABLE TO SPEAK TO OPERATOR:

> For the next few questions, we'd like you to think about the *people who operate or staff* the hotline and take calls.

IF ABLE TO SPEAK TO OPERATOR, ASK:

Q41. Does your office handle in-house the day-to-day operation and staffing of the operators who take hotline calls or do you outsource some, most or all of the staffing of the hotline staff to another company or organization?
  1. Handle day-to-day operation and staffing completely in-house
  2. Outsourced some of the day-to-day operation and staffing
  3. Outsourced most of the day-to-day operation and staffing
  4. Outsourced all of the day-to-day operation and staffing
  9. (No answer)

IF OUTSOURCE SOME, MOST or ALL, ASK:
Q42. How would you rate your satisfaction with this service provider?
  1. Very satisfied
  2. Somewhat satisfied
  3. Somewhat unsatisfied
  4. Very unsatisfied
  9. (No answer)

IF ABLE TO SPEAK TO OPERATOR, ASK:
Q43. During peak times or seasons what is the average number of full-time and part time hotline operators?
  _ _ _ full-time
  _ _ _ part-time
  9998 Not sure
  9999 (No answer)

IF ABLE TO SPEAK TO OPERATOR, ASK:
Q44. During non-peak peak times or seasons what is the average number of full-time and part time hotline operators?
  _ _ _ full-time
  _ _ _ part-time
  9998 Not sure
  9999 (No answer)

IF ABLE TO SPEAK TO OPERATOR, ASK:
Q45. For each of the following, please indicate whether or not this method is used to train hotline operators:

	Used	Not used	Not sure / Not enough information to answer	(No answer)
Classroom lectures	1	2	8	9
Role playing / simulated calls	1	2	8	9
Computer-based tutorial	1	2	8	9
Shadowing experienced operator or person	1	2	8	9

IF ABLE TO SPEAK TO OPERATOR, ASK:

Q46. Are all operators, regardless of their level of experience, trained before each major election cycle?

1. Yes
2. No
9. (No answer)

IF ABLE TO SPEAK TO OPERATOR, ASK:

Q47. Switching topics, what, if any, systematic effort does your office undertake to monitor the hotline for accuracy, security, or other critical performance variables?

	Yes	No	Not sure / Not enough information to answer	(No answer)
Periodic listening in on calls	1	2	8	9
Tracking of complaints	1	2	8	9
Other (please describe)	1	2	8	9

Q48. When a voter calls the hotline seeking information such as voting location, absentee ballot request, change of address, do you have a standardized procedure for verifying the caller's identity such as verifying social security number, date of birth, etc?

1. Yes, always
2. Yes, sometimes
3. No
9. (No answer)

Q49. Which, if any of the following security measures do you employ?

	Yes	No	Not enough information to answer	(No answer)
The data utilized by the hotline(s) is secured behind a firewall.	1	2	3	9
Operators need a secure password to access	1	2	3	9

Voter Information Websites Study

data.				

Q50. Thinking now about possible outreach efforts, what methods, if any, do you use to inform voters about our voter hotline?

	Use	Don't use	(No answer)
Advertise number in election mailing/sample ballot	1	2	9
Publicize number on office's or jurisdiction's website	1	2	9
Ads in local or community paper	1	2	9
Phone company operator	1	2	9
Handouts or posters at polling place	1	2	9
Advertise through outreach partners			

Q51. Last year, approximately how much did you spend specifically on publicizing your office's hotline(s)?

_____ USD

9999 (No answer)

We have just a few more questions to help us better understand the types of election offices taking part in our survey.

Q52. How many full-time and part-time staff work in your election office?

_____ full-time

_____ part-time 9999 (No answer)

Q53. Approximately how many voters are in your jurisdiction?

_____ [7-digit numeric response]

9 (No answer)

Q54. How would you describe the area of your jurisdiction?
1. Mainly rural
2. Mainly urban
3. Mainly suburban
4. Mixed
9. (No answer)

Q55. About what percentage of the voters in your area would you say are well-off, about average, and poorer than average? (just your best guess is fine)

_____ % well-off

_____ % about average

_____ % poorer than average

9999 (No answer)

Q56. About what percentage of the voters in your jurisdiction have a limited English proficiency? (just your best guess is fine)

110   U.S. Election Assistance Commission

_ _ _ %
9999 (No answer)

Q57. If your office *required* by federal law to publish election materials in a language other than English?
1. Yes
2. No
9. (No answer)

Q58. The EAC would like to collect the phone numbers of election-related phone information hotlines to publish on the EAC's website. If you consent to have your hotline number(s) given to the EAC, please provide the numbers below. By doing so, the EAC will know your office has responded to the survey, but they will NOT have the ability to connect your answers to you or your office. Your answers to all other questions will be combined with the responses of others who have taken the survey and will be reported in the aggregate to get an overall picture.

Voter hotlines:

_ _ _ - _ _ _ - _ _ _ _
_ _ _ - _ _ _ - _ _ _ _
_ _ _ - _ _ _ - _ _ _ _

Pollworker hotlines

_ _ _ - _ _ _ - _ _ _ _
_ _ _ - _ _ _ - _ _ _ _
_ _ _ - _ _ _ - _ _ _ _

Q59. Would you be willing to speak with one of our project researchers about your office's experience with phone information hotlines?
1. Yes
2. No
9. (No answer)

IF WILLING TO BE CONTACTED, ASK:
Q60. Please fill in your contact information below:
First name:
Last name:
Phone number:
Email:

*This information collection is required for the EAC to meet its statutory requirements under the Help America Vote Act (HAVA) of 2002 (42 U.S.C. 15301). Respondent's obligation to reply to this information collection is voluntary; respondents include election offices in the 50 States and the District of Columbia. This information will be made publicly available on the EAC website at www.eac.gov. According to the Paperwork Reduction Act of 1995, an agency may not conduct or sponsor, and a person is not required to respond to, a collection of information unless it displays a valid OMB control number. The valid OMB control number for this information collection is OMB Control No. pending (expires: to be determined). The time required to complete this information collection is estimated to average 30 minutes per response. Comments regarding this burden estimate should be sent to the Program Manager – 2007 Study of the Voter Hotlines, U.S. Election Assistance Commission, 1225 New York Ave, NW, Suite 1100, Washington, DC 20005

In: Voting Alternatives, Hotlines and Websites
Editors: Sean M. Thomas, and Daniel P. Allton

ISBN: 978-1-61324-593-4
© 2011 Nova Science Publishers, Inc.

Chapter 3

VOTER INFORMATION WEBSITES STUDY

U.S. Election Assistance Commission

INTRODUCTION

Section 245(a) of the Help America Vote Act (HAVA) mandates that the U.S. Election Assistance Commission (EAC) conduct a thorough study of issues and challenges presented by incorporating communications and Internet technologies. Section 245(a)(2)(C) indicates that the EAC may investigate the impact that new communications or Internet technology systems in the electoral process have on voter participation rates, voter education, and public accessibility. In addition, Section 241(b)(9) allows the EAC to periodically study election administration issues, including methods of educating voters on all aspects of voter participation.

Since the 1990s, pioneers in the election community have utilized the Internet to post voter and election information. Many of the approaches have produced impressive results and important insights, including making elections more efficient; but posting voter information on the Internet may have unintended consequences as well.

Early election websites focused on providing static information about the election process, voter registration, or election night results. Voters were often presented with a large amount of information and were expected to filter out inapplicable information themselves – a sometimes overwhelming task. As a result, these websites evolved from providing static election information to presenting dynamic and customized information for and about an individual voter.

This study is based on a review of active voter information websites in the fall of 2005 through 2006, from which 71 sites were identified as voter information websites and selected for in- depth analysis. Common functions of these websites were cataloged and quantified and presented to a panel of experts for discussion and review. The EAC's goal in undertaking this study is to provide guidelines that will assist election administrators in developing Voter Information websites that best serve voters.

Deciding *what* information to provide and *how* to provide it is the most important step in developing a voter information website because the information and method of delivery define the implementation process. The recommendations that follow outline key considerations that can be referenced when election officials consider constructing a voter information website. The suggestions can be used as a how-to guide to assist in developing new projects, or as a reference point for established projects.

SUMMARY OF FINDINGS

In interviews with election officials and the information technology (IT) professionals working for election jurisdictions, some distinct patterns emerged in the development of voter information websites. Projects that were developed with dedicated time and thoughtful consideration stood out. Likewise, projects that came together as add-ons to existing sites rarely received high marks. Many of the projects at the focus of this study were created as a result of use of the Internet and associated technologies in daily operations. The development of computerized voter registration lists and the software to maintain them, removed the barrier to creating a database that a Voter Information website can query.

This change lent itself to the development of voter information websites that were primarily voter registration look-ups. These provided election officials with state-wide access the basic utilities for per-voter reporting required so that election officials could answer the basic question, "Am I registered to vote?" from the authoritative database. A natural progression was to provide voters with the ability to use their Web browser to answer the question themselves.

Several officials commented that voter information websites have reduced calls to the election department on Election Day. Increase in traffic and frequency of lookups against the voter registration database were also cited as evidence of the popularity of the website. Many websites that provided voter registration took the next step to provide voters with ballot information specific to their jurisdiction. Those that did provide voters with information on candidates and contests increased usage of their website.

As voter information websites progress from voter registration lookup to interactive sample ballots, the complexity of the website and its relevance to the voting public increases. Growing public acceptance of these websites as a main source of voter information increases demand and raises expectations.

Additional features make a website more complex, and with complexity challenges that arise. As websites become more popular, there are greater possible usability or privacy issues that arise. A popular website can also strain under heavy usage during high-profile races, perfor-mance issues can occur when election officials can least afford them, and planning is required to anticipate spikes. Once voters have grown accustomed to the voter information website, and have integrated it into the routine they follow at each election, election bureaus may have to field calls about uptime and availability.

Well designed and implemented websites can bring in many more users. More users mean more voters will find answers online. If a regular visit to the election jurisdiction's website is part of a voter's routine, voters are more likely to assist in the maintenance of voter rolls by checking their registration. A popular and informative voter information website can be an invaluable tool for a jurisdiction to inform voters of changes to election procedures, voting equipment, polling locations, and to encourage informed participation.

Section 1: Understanding the Audience

Overview

Understanding voters' interests is critical to effectively communicating with the voting public. A voter information website's utility may be tied to successfully pairing the information election administrators wish to distribute with information voters seek.

To better provide the most useful information, election administrators must understand the different concerns and common interests of the audiences that use voter information websites. Though some questions and concerns apply to all voters, there are concerns specific to subcategories of users. Key audiences break into seven common constituencies: Six categories of voters and two organizational categories.

The seven identified voter information website audiences to consider are:

Voters
First-time voters
Infrequent voters
Consistent voters
Voters with special circumstances
UOCAVA voters
Absentee voters

Organizations
Advocacy organizations and Campaigns
The Media

First-Time Voters
First-time voters require the whole gamut of election information, including any peculiarities of the election or registration process (e.g. first time voters must vote in person, etc.).

Infrequent Voters
Infrequent voters are generally unfamiliar with the election process, and may be concerned that their inactivity will result in de-registration. This group of voters may need to be refreshed on where to vote and whether or not they are still registered.

Voters with Special Circumstances
This group typically uses voter information websites to obtain contact information for local election officials. Accordingly, it is always important for these voters to have easy access to information like phone numbers, mailing addresses, and email addresses.

Consistent Voters
Because of their high interest in the voting process, consistent voters often rely on sources other than official voter information websites to obtain information on upcoming

elections. When consistent voters do use an information website, they are usually looking for additional information about an election, such as proposals and sample ballots.

Uocava Voters

UOCAVA voters' main concern is typically registration since these voters need to vote from their last official residence. In addition, UOCAVA voters need the ability to check sample ballot information and look for additional candidate information that may not be available from an overseas location. UOCAVA voters also have increased interest in the turnaround time for processing absentee ballot applications. Consequently, this group of voters may find utilities that track absentee ballot processing very useful.

Absentee Voters

Absentee voters want to participate in the election but cannot do so in person on Election Day. These voters need to know how to obtain and fill in an absentee ballot. Usually this can be done with static information (footnote def). In-country absentee ballot voters are often consistent voters, but because the absentee balloting process often takes place weeks before major media coverage, many absentee ballot voters may vote with less detailed information on the election. Absentee voters who hold their ballots until closer to the election greatly benefit from voter information websites that help them access local election information from distant locations.

Voter information websites can also assist absentee voters through the ability to remotely track the absentee ballot process, from application, to delivery, and final processing in order to quickly resolve postal or processing problems.

Organizations

Advocacy organizations and campaigns

Advocacy organizations and campaigns typically seek information such as bulk registration lists. Real-time access to such lists allows advocacy groups to verify new registrations as they progress. Advocacy groups may also use voter information websites to verify individual voter registrations—this study uncovered two websites that were specifically created to screen for irregularities in voter registrations. [1/2]

Media

Media outlets are generally eager to add voter information features to election coverage, but they are hesitant to allow users to leave their own websites. The benefit of partnering with media outlets is that it allows election administrators to reach a larger audience, but media outlets may prefer to display data differently than election administrators.

SECTION 2: COMMON VOTER CONCERNS

Overview

After reviewing the websites listed in Appendix D, several voter questions consistently emerged as important common voter concerns[3]:

- Am I registered to vote?
- Where do I vote?
- Who/What is on the ballot?
- How do I use voting equipment?
- Did my vote count?

Am I registered to vote? Voter registration lookup

The information returned by a voter registration lookup includes items located on a voter registration card, such as name, voting district, and party affiliation. Some lookup tools also include a history of attendance at the polls (but not a record of how they voted). Typically, a voter is required to process a voter registration lookup before a voter information website can display polling place location or sample ballots.

Where do I vote? Polling place lookup

Some polling place lookup utilities link the address of a polling place to a public mapping service such as Google Maps©, Yahoo! Maps© or MapQuest©. Several election departments also reference maps generated by internal Geographic Information Systems (GIS) departments. Keep in mind that an address search answers the question: "Where is the polling location near this ad-dress?" The only way to answer the question where do *I* vote is to reference a voter registration file.

Who/What is on the ballot? Sample ballots

A sample ballot presents voters with information that includes only those contests in which the voter will vote. Sample ballots can either be displayed as web pages or as documents (e.g. downloadable Microsoft Word or Adobe PDF format). These documents and/or Web pages represent the actual ballot style that the voter will see at the polling location.

Candidate Information

There are three main ways to supply candidate information: (1) official candidate statements collected by election administrators, (2) links to official candidate websites, and (3) links to third-party information sites, such as the League of Women Voters.

Candidate Statements

Collecting candidates' statements allows voters equal access to candidate messages and provides a benefit to candidates. As voter information websites become more widespread, it is likely that candidates will welcome the opportunity to provide statements on such sites.

U.S. Election Assistance Commission

Links to Candidates' Official Websites

One concern about linking to a candidate's website is that it may appear as though election administrators are endorsing one candidate or another. However, this can be alleviated by alerting users when a link takes them to an independent website.

Links to Third-Party Information

Similar to linking to candidates' official websites, election administrators should clearly alert users when they are being directed to websites hosted by third parties to avoid confusion concerning endorsements.

Other Ballot-Related Information

Many elections include initiatives, amendments, or referenda which are required to be worded as they would appear if adopted. Consequently, they often include official legal wording that may pose a challenge to voters with low literacy levels. To help clarify what a legal clause means or what effect it would have, voter information websites may want to provide links to explanations of the official language.

How do I use voting equipment?

Poll worker outreach and training campaigns are typically more effective tools for teaching voters how to use voting equipment than voter information websites. Voters commonly expect that voting equipment is either self-explanatory or someone at the polling place will assist users.

Provisional Ballots: Did my vote count?

HAVA requires states to provide voters with provisional ballots in certain circumstances. When elections are contested, one of the first areas contenders target are provisional votes. Conse-quently, it is advisable to create a utility where voters can verify that provisional ballots have been counted.

SECTION 3. PRELIMINARY PLANNING

Overview

Much of the information voters seek online is static and does not need to reference a database. For example, voter registration forms, absentee voting procedures, election dates, and results are critical components of election information websites, but they do not change over time and are not specific to the voter. Adding information specific to voters requires consideration of several factors that are not presented by static sites.

The first step in creating a voter information website is to decide what information will be posted on the site and how it will be displayed. The project outline for developing and implementing a voter information website will vary depending on these factors and the amount of information each site seeks to convey.[4]

Recommendation 3.1: Answer the Question "Am I registered to vote?"

This is one of the key questions voters ask on Election Day. Websites that do not attempt or are currently unable to answer this question will have limited efficacy. In addition, failing to answer this question may lead to third party organizations creating their own utilities to answer the question, reducing election administrators' ability to control accuracy.

Recommendation 3.2: Review legal considerations

Consider relevant laws and administrative rules that pertain to public access to voter information. If the law does not currently anticipate public access to voter information online, consult with legal counsel and legislators during the planning stage to ensure continued compliance with laws and rules.

Recommendation 3.3: Update voter records as often as possible

Due to security concerns outlined in detail in Section 6: Security and Privacy, the registry of record should not be exposed to the Internet. However, as a general rule to ensure accuracy, online records should be updated as often as they are changed on the registry of record. The frequency of updates will be dictated by volume, capacity, and proximity to Election Day. For example, in a jurisdiction with Election Day registration, having pre-existing registrations online on Election Day can greatly increase efficiency and decrease duplicate records

Recommendation 3.4: Adopt a neutral voice

The most useful voter information website is the one that is updated and maintained regularly during the campaign season by election administrators themselves. Voter information websites should be presented with a neutral voice, and should be absolutely free of candidate promotion.

Recommendation 3.5: Use Effective design principles

Some of the websites reviewed in this study provided useful information, but the designs made accessing information complicated.[5] A good website will present useful information in a simple and consistent format. This area of planning may be enhanced through the use of an expert consultant who can advise on industry standards. Further discussion on this subject can be found in Section 5: Accessibility.

Recommendation 3.6: Contract out work as needed

Depending on a jurisdiction's resources, IT staff may not have the breadth of knowledge or time to develop a web application internally. Reports from the websites studied indicated that in-house development hours were not regularly documented, and some cost estimates were un-der reported.[6] Deciding whether to contract out work also requires consideration of the avail-ability of internal staff during peak website usage times.

Recommendation 3.7: Review contractors' prior work

Although voter information websites are a relatively new specialty, it may be useful to consult experts when planning one. Some things to consider when selecting an expert are quality of service, average time websites are inoperable, availability of technicians, cost, and quality of work-product. For many of the websites reviewed in this study, election administrators and internal IT staff worked in concert, so that administrative, technological, and legal concerns could be integrated in the planning.

Recommendation 3.8: Consider commercial off-the-shelf (COTS) and open source solutions

None of the websites in this study used COTS or open source, but many used components of each. Reviewing available options will help ensure that whatever design method adopted conforms to state policy goals.

Recommendation 3.9: Establish clear goals before development

Determine the features of your voter information website during the planning process. Define your desired feature set before you begin development. Have a clear understanding of how you're going to collect the information necessary to build your voter information website before dedicating resources or hiring contractors.

Recommendation 3.10: Inventory data sources

Investigate current data sources and document their location, current file format, frequency of updates, and duplication. This will allow election administrators to coordinate information gathering and aggregating data from disparate sources.

Recommendation 3.11: Plan for high capacity peaks

Promoting a voter information website will increase the site's popularity, especially as Election Day approaches (See Section 5: Marketing and Promotion). Determine in advance if the bandwidth currently available will accommodate increased activities immediately before, during, and after Election Day. In addition, assess IT resources to enable emergent problems with the website to be efficiently resolved.

Recommendation 3.12: Consider intellectual property and copyright issues

Research websites that provide the capabilities each jurisdiction wishes to implement and determine if any of the products currently online are patented, copyrighted, or licensed. Consult with legal advisors to ensure compliance with applicable intellectual property and licensing laws.

Recommendation 3.13: Document project development and system functionality

At each stage of user interface design, project planners should develop and document context- sensitive helpful hints for users. Documenting this information will allow users to self-diagnose problems with the interface and can also serve as technical guidelines for election call center staff, who may be required to assist callers with the website. Documentation also serves to inform potential future staff and contractors who may be hired after the voter information website is developed.

Recommendation 3.14: Budget for development, hosting, capacity, and promotion

It is important when planning a voter information website to account for all resources involved, including production, design, bandwidth, maintenance, programming, data collection, and staff hours. Costs associated with sites that initially start as add-ons to preexisting voter registration databases must take into account changes and maintenance to systems over time. Sites that are built in-house should use time tracking tools to accurately assess staff hours involved. Further, although outside contractors generally track their own hours, election jurisdictions should also incorporate internal staff hours used to supplement contractor work.

In addition to planning and design costs, promotion can be a significant cost. Creating a voter information website and failing to promote it may leave it unused by the public. Investment in a voter information website should include a promotion campaign. The more a voter information website is promoted, the more voters will use it (correspondingly, it should be noted that the more traffic a website receives, the more it will cost to host). General guidelines and promotional considerations are discussed in Section 5: Marketing and Promotion of this report.

Recommendation 3.15: Track usage patterns

Using site-monitoring tools to observe usage patters is an indispensable tool in keeping a voter information website reflective of voter concerns and relevant. For example, site-monitoring tools can track how long users spend on each page, how they navigate the site, and how often files are downloaded. These patterns can change over time, so continual monitoring is advisable.

SECTION 4: FEATURES

Overview

The following list of features has been collected from various voter information websites across the country.[7] The features listed below answer questions outlined in Section 2: COMMON VOTER QUESTIONS.[8]

Recommendation 4.1: Provide voters with the answer to the question "Where do I vote?"

Websites that do not attempt to answer "Where do I vote?" have limited efficacy and will result in all voter questions concerning where to vote being routed to a state or local call center. In addition, not answering this question on a voter information website may encourage third party organizations to create their own websites, which can limit accuracy.

Keep in mind that an address search answers the question: "Where is the polling location near this address?" The only way to answer the question where do *I* vote is to reference a voter registration file. When answering this question, include the street address of the polling place. Some voter files do not provide complete street addresses for polling locations. Websites built on voter files that reference a polling location at a church or a school but do not include the address can make it difficult to plot on a map. If polling places change frequently between elections and the information is not always available, inform voters when the information will be available again.

Recommendation 4.2: Add map links to polling locations

Maps are a useful addition to the polling location identification information provided to voters. This is especially beneficial to new residents and when polling places are somewhat obscure. There are many competing services that provide great mapping services for free.[9]

Recommendation 4.3: Do not provide voters with driving directions

Driving directions pose a potential privacy and liability risk and could be an unnecessary distraction. Voters wishing to access directions to polling place locations would be better served to use dedicated mapping websites.

Recommendation 4.4: When including mapping programs, use the simplest versions available

Many of the websites reviewed in this study included mapping functions that did not seem directly relevant to polling place location. For example, the ability to zoom in and out of a map may not be necessary and could provide a distraction to voters looking for a general geographic orientation. In addition, more features mean more potential for confusion and technical dif-ficulties. The scale of polling place identification maps should be relatively consistent. Despite features that may be available (zoom-in, city view, 3D, etc.) through state geographical information systems (GIS), highlighting map capabilities over functionality is unnecessary. Be sensitive to avoid providing too much information or too many features.

Recommendation 4.5: Provide voters with a sample ballot

A Sample ballot is the most significant section of voter information website when measured by the time a voter spends reviewing information online. Polling location and registration data can be reviewed quickly; however, sample ballots, especially if linked to additional reference information, can take time to review. Jurisdictions contemplating a voter information website should consider including sample ballot display functionality in its site.

Recommendation 4.6: Display sample ballots exactly as they will appear on Election Day

Including information about races in multiple jurisdictions on a single sample ballot may confuse voters. The goal should be to provide voters with an exact replica of what they will see on Election Day. Voters can react negatively when presented with too much information

Recommendation 4.7: Link sample ballots to helpful information

The most popular feature of the more mature voter information websites studied were "interactive sample ballots."[10] An interactive sample ballot is a ballot that has been tailored to a specific voter, and provides links to additional information about candidates and proposals. In many cases, these links are to pre-existing published non-partisan voter guides, but they can also be links to campaign websites, campaign finance information and other non-partisan sources. The few sites across the country that have built interactivity into sample ballots have tracked strong user popularity.

Voter Information Websites Study

Recommendation 4.8: Do not link to incumbent government websites on a voter guide
Linking a sample ballot to an incumbent's official government-funded website may persuade voters that election administrators are biased or that incumbents are using shared resources to their benefit.

Recommendation 4.9: Give voters the ability to track absentee ballots online
A few voter information websites reviewed in this study included the ability to check the status of an absentee ballot application.[11] The ability to follow the absentee ballot process is especially critical to overseas and military voters.

Recommendation 4.10: Allow users to check the status of provisional ballots online
The websites in this study were primarily focused on delivering voter-specific information prior to an election. The ability to verify the status of a provisional ballot is one voter-specific postelection function that few websites performed.[12] Given the provisions in HAVA that require notification of the status of a provisional ballot, voter information websites provide an easy solution to communicating with voters concerning provisional ballots while lessening the burden on election administrators.

Recommendation 4.11: Provide instructions for how to use voting equipment
Providing information on how to use voting equipment is valuable when there are changes to voting equipment. In addition, providing instructions allows new voters and voters new to the jurisdiction with information that can help alleviate wait times on Election Day. In addition to static files, (word, PDF), interactive examples and videos are good resources as well.

Recommendation 4.12: Post Election Day times and polling location hours prominently
While a single election calendar can cover an entire voting population, do not miss any opportunity to remind voters of these important dates and times.

Recommendation 4.13: Provide other readily-available information neatly and in a logical manner
This list of features is not exhaustive, and there have been many instances of other information presented through a voter registry lookup, such as candidate specific campaign finance information, and disability access. Present other information where it makes sense.

SECTION 5: MARKETING AND PROMOTION

Overview

There is a direct relationship between how much promotion a voter information website receives and the capacity such a site has to accommodate immediately prior to Election Day.

In nearly every website studied that tracked usage patterns, basic voter usage remained consistent, but a marked increase was noted on or around Election Day. Accordingly, election administrators must address the following issues:

1. How much will the website be promoted?
2. How much traffic should each jurisdiction anticipate?

In the course of reviewing websites for this study, two patterns emerged. First, voter information websites were part of a larger outreach campaign, such as a public service announcement. The other approach used the voter information website as the central point of distribution for election information. The second approach likely maximizes traffic to voter information websites.

Recommendation 5.1: Consider different user audiences in promoting a voter information website

Understanding the audience of voter information websites is a key to the success of your voter information website. See Section 1: UNDERSTANDING THE AUDIENCE Understanding the Audience, for a breakdown of voter interest categories. There is limited demographic information available concerning usage of voter information websites. However, general trends showing the demographics of the users of the Internet indicate that Internet use shoots up in younger Americans.[13]

Recommendation 5.2: Repetition equals reinforcement

The single most effective way to promote a voter information website is to reinforce the connection between voter questions and relevant information on a jurisdiction's voter information website.

Recommendation 5.3: Use traditional media to promote voter information websites

While it is possible to advertise on the Internet, the same principles that apply to political campaigns can help promote voter information websites. Traditional media- radio, television and print advertising can be critical to increase awareness of your services and drive users to your website.

Recommendation 5.4: Include your voter information website address on all voter out-reach and election materials

Any form of voter outreach by election officials and staff should include reference to a voter information website. In addition, it is a good idea when giving interviews to mention the website's address whenever possible.

Recommendation 5.5: Encourage election staff to direct voters to the voter information website

Encourage election staff (and Secretaries of State or chief election officials) to mention the voter information website as a resource to anyone who asks for information. The amount of traffic you get on the website will vary depending on how much you promote it and how effective your promotion is

Recommendation 5.6: Adjust your capacity to account for your promotion

The amount of traffic on a voter information website will vary depending on how much promotion it receives and how effective the promotion was. During peak times, voter informa-tion websites can become inundated with users, while off-peak times may result in few users. Election jurisdictions should plan to meet the high demand times as necessary, without taxing resources too heavily during low demand times.

Recommendation 5.7: Identify and consider factors that may increase traffic

Examples of some factors that may increase traffic are voting age population, popularity of the Internet, and the presence of a college or university within a jurisdiction. As each jurisdiction is different, election administrators should take into account who might be using the site and how demographics may influence usage.

Recommendation 5.8: Make voter information website addresses simple and easy to remember

Many states still have complicated Web addresses. This can be a problem when working a quick reference into an interview, or when a voter tries to recall a voter information website they've heard on the radio. Whatever website address an election jurisdiction chooses should be easy to remember.

There is not enough empirical data to conclusively recommend for or against using a distinct URL. There is an obvious communication advantage to *"statevotes.com"* over "www.state. st.us/departments/elections/vote" but statevotes.com can also easily be confused with "statevotes.org" which could be a website set up by spammers or spoofers. A ".gov" address may help clarify ownership, but as a precaution, any site that uses domains other than .com address should also purchase the corresponding .com and .org addresses. In order to avoid voters accessing incorrect or deliberately misleading information created by outside parties.

Recommendation 5.9: Build promotion around a single website address

Some proposed models of voter information website design include modular components of statewide systems that are available for use by local jurisdictions. While this allows local jurisdictions flexibility, exposures to multiple official website addresses is also confusing.

Recommendation 5.10: Allow official voter information websites to be used as a tool for local voter outreach programs

Don't underestimate the value a voter information website can have for third party organizations preparing voters for elections, and the benefit such partnerships may present to election jurisdictions. A Web address that is shared across multiple jurisdictions can be especially useful to third-party organizations that often operate in multiple jurisdictions.

Section 6. Security and Privacy

Overview

Voter information websites allow access to potentially sensitive information and should be carefully constructed to avoid jeopardizing privacy voters or the integrity and security of the records. Voter information can be compromised by falling into the wrong hands or by being modified to the detriment of accuracy. This section is divided into a discussion of concerns of the privacy of a voter and the security of the website.

The Privacy of an individual voter's record sparked debate during workgroup discussions. There are two schools of thought on the distribution of public information. Because voter registration records are public, it is legal to distribute this information without considering individual privacy. Still, few voters consider the first name, last name, middle name, city of residence, street address and birthday "public" information.

Privacy on the Internet is a high-profile concern in the public consciousness. The fear of exposure to fraud and identity theft inhibits many people from supplying what appears to be personal information.

A voter information website assumes a single voter as the target user. Website language was directed at "you" the voter and the information supplied, registration status, polling locations, disability access, sample ballots, etc, are intended to promote an efficient election day voting experience. When voter information websites begin to combine purposes it is often at the peril of a voter's personal privacy and security.

In general, a succinct transaction seems to be the most secure and efficient method of distributing information about an individual voter. This approach requires voter information web- sites to ask only for information absolutely needed to complete the request and return only the information a voter absolutely needs. The total information exchanged on a voter information website, input and output, should be as brief as possible, to protect the integrity of the election and the interests of individual voters.

Recommendations in this section are followed by what is threatened in parenthesis.

6.1. EAC Recommendation: Do Not Expose the Official Registry File to the Internet (*official voter registry file security*)

Information that is available on the Internet is exposed to threats of tampering; computers exposed to the Internet are exposed to denial of service attacks and the threat of intrusion. Create a copy of your authoritative database to use for your voter information website and regularly update it from the authoritative database. No one should ever be able to change a voter's official status by compromising a website.

Security of a voter information website should be maintained and revisited over time. If a voter information website is tampered with, a voter may receive inaccurate information. Regular verification of the accuracy of the data in your exposed database is advised.

6.2. EAC Recommendation: Do not Expose Data to the Internet that Is not Used by Your Voter Information Website *(unused registry data security)*

This recommendation applies to the security of information that may be in the exposed registry file, but not used in the online transaction. Sensitive data such as driver's license numbers shouldn't be exposed on the Internet if they are not necessary to the function of the website, and application developers should work to avoid using such information. When creating the database that will be accessed online, unnecessary information should be removed completely, not left in place.

6.3. EAC Recommendation: Avoid Asking for Too Much Information *(online transaction security)*

Online voter searches should be as efficient as possible. Determine and use the absolute minimum amount of information necessary to accurately identify a voter record. Unnecessary information uses resources. Consider the wasted time, computational cycles, database queries and user attention it takes to input and process six data points for every voter if three will suffice.

Websites that ask for excessive information can deter usage for other reasons. If a website asks too many question end users may avoid it because it seems onerous. Given the increase in identity related crime, users may also be apprehensive about divulging "personal"[14] information over the Internet and asking for too much information may seem invasive to the user and deter use. Election administrators should be judicious when asking for information. Even if information is technically not private, it is not safe to assume that all voters consider their name, address, and birth date open to anonymous online consumption as a matter of public record.

Asking for too much information poses another potential risk. While it seems logical that the more information that can be verified, the greater the accuracy, the possibility exists that identity thieves could set out to collect information about a voter by creating a fake voter information website.[15]

6.4. EAC Recommendation: Review and Comply with Your Jurisdiction's Security Policies on Encrypting Data *(online transaction security)*

Review your web policies on passing data through an encrypted connection. When asked, many of the web administrators cited that the information "was public anyway." If a voter information website limits the amount of data requested and granted, the necessity of encryption in this context is arguable, but does not appear to be harmful.

6.5. EAC Recommendation: Make Sure You Know Who is Working with Your Voter Information *(web development security and individual voter privacy)*

Chain of custody is important when dealing with voter registry data. Determine if you will use contractors and who within your organization will spearhead the project. Establish clear boundaries between tasks required of your internal IT department and those of your contractors. Know the chain of custody of your data. If contractors are going to be handling sensitive information, make sure they understand the liability and have a proven track record of security. Review policies on the use of outsourced and overseas contractors when handling sensitive voter data.

6.6. EAC Recommendation: Use Increased Security if You Set Out to Vet the Voter Registry for Accuracy, and Avoid Doing so at the Expense of Voter Security. *(online transaction security and individual voter privacy)*

This recommendation applies to the security of the online transaction and voter privacy. One side of the privacy discussion contends that since voter registration information is public, people are safer if they know that it is available. In addition, the integrity of the voter registration file is enhanced when voters can verify and correct information in the file. This perspective has additional weight when viewed through the lens of states that rely heavily on mail-in balloting. Correct addresses in a mail-in ballot system may affect whether a voter receives a ballot without soliciting one. Advocacy groups have also expressed interest in the publication of addresses to aid in voter registration activities. Address verification required to maintain accurate registration files should be conducted as securely as possible, separate from the ability to verify registration on a voter information website. Unless effort has been made to authenticate a user, it is impossible to keep information about voters in one locality from being accessible everywhere. If a voter information website is designed to be a tool for vetting voter addresses to increase accuracy, it can be at the expense of voter privacy.

Although this school of thought raises important and legitimate concerns, they are not necessarily the provenance of voter information websites. Public access to voter records is necessary as a check on the integrity of the election, but anonymous public access to all data in a record is not necessary to prepare an individual voter for an election. Concern for the safety of voters through unregulated anonymous access to voter records is considerable, as is the potential damage done by identity theft. [16]

6.7. EAC Recommendation: Display as Little Information as Possible about the Voter - Just Enough to Answer the Voter's Question *(online transaction security and individual voter privacy)*

A voter registration website should reveal as little as possible about individual voters. While a voter information website can serve as a tool to check the accuracy of voter records, the public right to inspect voter records can be achieved through official documented request, and therefore does not need to be a primary design consideration.

The goal of limiting disclosure is to provide the voter with accurate information while limiting access to information useful to potential wrongdoers. Make sure you review your website to determine if it poses a threat to voters, or the election process. The key to protecting voters and the integrity of the election when creating a voter information website is to carefully review the questions to be asked and the answers received.

6.8. EAC Recommendation: Avoid Disclosing a Voter's Birth Date or Current Address *(individual voter privacy and security)*

A voter information website that displays a voter's birth data or address can inadvertently facilitate criminal activity because it is anonymous, and available anywhere, anytime. Although voter addresses and birthdates are public, entering a government office and documenting a request for an individual voter's information is more involved and can be traced. Most voters recognize if a polling location is near a current or former address, and can confirm "is this in your neighborhood?" Allowing unfettered access to names, addresses and birth dates, is an invitation to abuse them.

6.9. EAC Recommendation: Make Sure Your Website is Not a Stalking Tool *(individual voter privacy and security)*

A stalker uses any means available to locate a target, and an anonymously accessible online voter registration file can be a valuable resource. Many states offer stalking victims the op-tion to redact their personal information from publicly accessible registration lists[17], but to use these programs the voter must opt-in. Since individuals must be aware of potential threats before they can request participation in a redaction program relying on this approach alone leaves voter information exposed for anyone who does not know he or she has been targeted. It is safer to avoid exposing address information.

6.10. EAC Recommendation: Review You Website to Make Sure it is Not Useful for Identity Theft *(individual voter privacy and security)*

This recommendation applies to voter privacy and security. Every voter is a potential target of identity theft at any time. Examine how much voter information is disclosed and hypothetically consider if an identity thief used your website, how much information could they obtain and what could be done with it? Armed with a name, address and a birth date, a criminal could easily pursue further information for purposes of obtaining financial records or other information. Name, address and birth date alone may not be sufficient to cause harm, they are starting points for "phishing"[18] and "pretexting"[19], or other social engineering schemes.

6.11. EAC Recommendation: Make Sure Your Website Does Not Facilitate Election Fraud (*election security*)

Anonymous access to the names, addresses and birth dates of infrequent voters could be the basis for sophisticated Election Day fraud.

6.12. EAC Recommendation: Use Implied Information When Possible (*individual voter privacy and transaction security*)

A valuable method of supplying information without exposing excess information is implied information. Election authorities have all the information in a voter's record so it is possible to design website queries to leverage the information on file without divulging it. An example of implied information: if a voter's identity is confirmed and matches a registration record, that voter's polling location is displayed; if the voter's identity does not match a registration record, the voter is informed that he or she is not registered. The voter is never told explicitly that he or she is registered, but may deduce from the result of a polling location search whether or not that is the case. This approach can be described symbolically as:

if registered = true then display = polling location
if registered = false then display = not registered

The scenario: *if registered = true then display = registered* does not need to be displayed. (*Registered* is a characteristic of a voter, whereas *polling location* is an independent data object, generally considered "public" information.) Registration is implied, and by eliminating its display, fewer characteristics of the actual voter are divulged, while the voter still has the necessary information to vote.

In another example, data itself can be confirmed without exposure to the user. A jurisdiction's registrar's office already possesses each voter's name, address and birth date. An address can be verified by the user supplying a street address number, rather than the site displaying the entire address for the user to select. If the street numbers submitted match the registrar's record, then the address can be verified:

if input = 12345 Street and record = 12345 Street then display = polling location
if input = 12345 Street and record = 56789 Street then display = contact your registrar

In this case the address record is validated and no additional information about the voter is displayed to the user who inputs the data. There may be special circumstances that apply to specific voters, such as a requirement to vote in person. Take care when displaying information about voters. Depending on the sensitivity of the information, you may want to consider a separate authenticated login.

6.13. EAC Recommendation: Avoid Displaying Information about More than One Voter *(individual voter privacy and transaction security)*

The opposite of a limited disclosure approach might be termed a "multiple disclosure" approach. Multiple disclosures go beyond limited and full disclosures to expose information about more than one voter per query. An example of this type of voter information website implementation would be identifying all voters in residence at a specific address. The site might request the input of an address and display information on the names of the registered voters at the input address:

if input = 12345 Street then display = voter 1 name, voter 2 name, voter 3 name

Thus, a user in possession of only an address can find information about multiple voters. An entire apartment building could be exposed in such a case.

6.14. EAC Recommendation: Avoid Using Lists *(individual voter privacy and transaction security)*

This recommendation applies to voter privacy and transaction security. There is no need to expose more than one voter's information to anyone using the site. Refer to the section in this document on Privacy for more details.

Similarly, using a list to confirm a voter's identity should be discouraged:

if input = John Smith then display = did you mean:
John Smith at 12345 Street in City X
John Smith at 56789 Street in City X
John Smith at 45678 Street in City Y
John Smith at 54321 Street in Town Z

Here, information for all John Smiths in this particular jurisdiction is exposed.

6.15. EAC Recommendation: Avoid Information Over-Exposure *(individual voter privacy)*

This recommendation applies to voter privacy and transaction security. Secondary clarification prevents the need to manually filter multiple results. A secondary question like: *"What city town or village do you live in?"* or *"What is your middle initial?"* can clarify a voter's identity without exposing it.

if input = John Smith then display = What city, town or village do you live in?
if input = City X and record = City X then display = polling location
if input = Town Z and record = City X then display = contact your registrar

6.16. EAC Recommendation: Avoid Asking for Obscure Information *(online transaction security)*

This recommendation applies to transaction security. Sites can disrupt the flow of a smooth user experience by asking for information outside of what is expected. Election administrators should be careful to keep the information requested within the end user's understanding of the transaction. Requesting obscure information can be impractical for two reasons: if the information requested is difficult to immediately recall, a user may get frustrated and stop. It is not uncommon for sites to ask for a driver's license number, zip+4 , voter ID, DMV ID, or even a specially requested PIN personal identification number; however, doing so forces the user to search for that information before they can obtain information they seek. You may only get one chance at delivering information to a voter online; you don't want to turn them away.

SECTION 7: DESIGNING A POSTIVE USER EXPERIENCE

Overview

Websites must take into account the flow of information from page to page- the "user experience". A good user experience is critical to the success of a voter information website as it will encourage repeat users and positive word-of-mouth advertisement. A positive user experience is designed with the end-user in mind.

Poor design and complicated layout can deter usage. Common functions should be grouped in high visibility locations, and more obscure or detailed information can be in lower profile locations deeper into the site for committed users, or users seeking answers to very specific questions. In general, simplicity is the key. Voter information Websites should use pictographic artifacts wherever possible to avoid excessive reliance on text.

Crafting the user experience is one of the areas where outside design experts may be a valu-able resource. There is also a wealth of user interface research available online, detailing good design practices for page layout and navigation. Two U.S. Government sites that have already addressed Web design and usability for government-related applications are the U.S. Department of Health and Human Services' www.usability.gov and the General Services Administration's www.webcontent.gov.

Recommendation 7.1: Move users quickly from general to specific information

Move from the general to the specific in your information architecture. Different users will access voter information websites for different reasons. It is imperative that voter informa-tion websites move users quickly to the information they require so that users don't navigate elsewhere.

As an example, not every voter will be a first time voter, so a voter information website should avoid asking every visitor if they are a first time voter. Most website users will not belong to a specialized category, so emphasize these options as alternate branches off the main path a voter will navigate through, not as obstacles. No one wants to fill out a detailed questionnaire before they begin to use the system.

Recommendation 7.2: Employ industry standard graphic design principles and highlight the most popular features

Graphic design, layout and intuitive flow of the user experience are in their respective industries scientific disciplines. There are experts in the field that can advise election jurisdictions about the most effective way to display material. Awkward design and layout were very common among the websites studied. While there is no one standard format for voter information websites, voters should easily see what information they will be able to access on a voter information website.

Recommendation 7.3: Review design to ensure simplicity

User interface design can take place parallel to the database and software development. The key concern is whether or not information is logical and available where users expect it. Watch people use the site – often small assumptions at this stage can result in major user frustration in the end product. The user interface should be tested for use on multiple browser platforms and operating systems. Usability testing should be run on static mock-ups of the website.

Recommendation 7.4: use broad and simple language; link to legal detail as necessary

Election laws can be complicated especially when every variable and scenario is fully documented. Voter information websites need only display broad concepts and do not need to be presented in full legal detail. When complicated concepts are unavoidable, consider whether an interactive narrated experience can help users navigate. For example:

Are you a first time voter? YES > Are you a student? YES > Did you register in person? etc.

Review the section on Accessibility in this document for a summary of reading comprehension levels and simple, clear and accessible language.

Recommendation 7.5: Encourage voters with complex questions to contact election ad-ministrators

Even when a voter's question cannot be anticipated, it is still possible to provide voters with the means to ask those questions directly. Besides phone numbers, providing email addresses and Web forms for voters to submit questions in their own words can assist election administrators in effectively addressing voters' needs.

Recommendation 7.6: Use clear and consistent menus and icons

Graphic elements can assist with website legibility and usability. Development of a set of "common language icons" consistently used throughout the site, will contribute to users' sense of familiarity while researching information.

Recommendation 7.7: Use simple and recognizable visual language

Decreasing text and emphasizing easily identifiable graphics can help users establish *where* and *how* to obtain information and/or move to the next step. Buttons or similar elements that enact a behavior, such as visually depressing when clicked, enhance users' understanding. An excess of graphics, however, can slow response times considerably during peak usage. Where graphics are not required for navigation or other essential uses, text-based alternatives should also be made available. Also, all graphics should make use of alt text for compatibility with speaking browsers (a Section 508 requirement).

Recommendation 7.8: Avoid excessive graphic design

Poor or awkward design can be a hallmark of an underused website. Because election administrators cannot pre-determine what equipment is used to visit a voter information website, the design and layout should be simple and readable by as many computer and software variations as possible. Confusion or discomfort with voter information websites not only limits what the voter gains by using the site, but may deter further use.

Recommendation 7.9: Use "Frequently Asked Questions"

To address multiple scenarios without overwhelming voters, using "Frequently Asked Questions" pages and links that move from general questions (e.g. "Are you a first-time voter?", "Do you have a drivers' license or state ID?") to more specific is helpful.

Recommendation 7.10: Avoid asking voters for information that is not readily-available

Many people don't have their driver's license number or Zip +4 memorized, for example. Asking such questions may deter users from further navigating on a voter information website.

SECTION 8: ACCESSIBILITY

Overview

Accessibility addresses compliance with Section 508 of the Rehabilitation Act of 1973. It also encompasses emerging technologies intended to enhance user experiences, designing clear user interfaces, designing for people whose first language isn't English, and designing for people with limited literacy or Internet experience. For example, voters who access the Internet through a public library or community library may not have the permission or ability to install special software or browser plug-ins such as Flash or Adobe Reader.

Recommendation 8.1: Establish section 508 as a minimum requirement for usability

Section 508 of the Rehabilitation Act of 1973 requires that federal agencies make their websites accessible to persons with disabilities. Subpart B, 1194.22 of Section 508 sets out standards for website compliance, which are located at: *www.section508.gov.* The United States Access Board is the federal agency that developed the accessibility standards; a standards guide, frequently asked questions, and other resources are available on the Board's website at: *www. access.*

Although Section 508 dictates accessibility for users with disabilities, 508 requirements still may not address usability for all users. Therefore, it is advisable that election jurisdictions implement usability testing, which aims at designing the most practical and easy to use website.

Recommendation 8.2: Follow foreign language requirements for printed materials on the website

Many jurisdictions have significant populations for whom English is a second language. In designing a voter information website, election jurisdictions should apply federal, state, and local laws regarding printed material translation equally to online content.

Recommendation 8.3: Ensure that content is written at a basic or intermediate literacy level

Functional literacy is measured in gradations by The National Assessment of Adult Literacy (NAAL). NAAL was conducted in 2003 by the U.S. Department of Education to measure English literacy in American adults.[20] The 500 point NAAL scoring system was separated into four ranges: Below Basic, Basic, Intermediate and Proficient. In 2003, the average Document Literacy score for all adults fell within the Intermediate range. More resources are available at: www.nces.ed.gov.

Except where specific wording is legally required, written material should not exceed a standard appropriate for the Intermediate level. In addition, since roughly 1 in 5 adults read at the Basic level and 1 in 7 read at Below Basic, use of "short, commonplace prose text" wherever possible is appropriate.

Recommendation 8.4: Ensure that website design encompasses users of below-average Internet literacy

To accommodate users who may not be familiar with the Internet or have regular access to it, voter information websites should make user interfaces as open as possible so that access to information does not require changes to browser settings or personalization. Voter information websites should not require specific browsers, restrict usage by requiring specific software, or depend on browser features such as cookies or JavaScript to operate properly.

Recommendation 8.5: Ensure compliance with new technologies when designing a voter information website

As access to the Internet continues to grow, users may access voter information websites from PDAs or cell phones. Some of these other forms of access require new considerations such as how their browsers render sites, and what sorts of input mechanisms they allow. Voter information websites should plan for compatibility with different Internet-ready devices because variously-sized display areas, limited input devices, and proprietary browsers will pose an ongoing design challenge to voter information websites.

Recommendation 8.6: Use simple technologies

To guarantee access to voters who use shared computers, limit the use of plug-in technologies that require administrative privileges to install. In addition, election jurisdictions should limit website features that require frequent browser upgrades or special software to operate correctly.

As an example, Adobe Reader is a common browser plug-in used to read Adobe PDF files, but it may not be installed on every computer. If a sample ballot is presented only in PDF format and a voter is using a shared computer without the appropriate software, he or she may not be able to view the ballot. On the other hand, if a voter information database can provide a HTML representation of the ballot, all users will be able to view the ballot.

Recommendation 8.7: Display pages in printer-friendly formats

Printable sample ballots, legible maps of polling places, and short biographies or statements by candidates (in districts where those are supplied) can be saved and/or printed by users who do not have ready access to the Internet, increasing their efficacy. In addition, creating Web pages in printer-friendly formats further allow third party organizations to help election jurisdictions inform voters by passing out information directly from a voter information website.

Recommendation 8.8: Indicate Polling Location Accessibility Information

Whenever possible, polling place information should include details about accessibility such as identifying entrances with ramp access or where elevators are located.

APPENDIX A. STUDY BACKGROUND AND METHODOLOGY

HAVA Mandate

In June of 2005, staff at the U.S. Election Assistance Commission (EAC) undertook a survey of public access portals available online to determine trends in voter questions and what entities were sponsoring online portals. The EAC found that there were several public access portals in operation for the 2004 Presidential election. Sponsorship ranged from locally-based governments to the independent sector and private corporations. Many of the websites were found to be duplicative, disorganized, and often erroneous. The EAC also found that voters primarily wanted two questions answered on Election Day: (1) Am I registered? and (2) Where do I vote?

Section 245(a) of the Help America Vote Act (HAVA) mandates that the U.S. Election Assistance Commission (EAC) conduct a thorough study of issues and challenges presented by incorporating communications and Internet technologies. Section 245(a)(2)(C) indicates that the EAC may investigate the impact that new communications or Internet technology systems in the electoral process have on voter participation rates, voter education, and public accessibility. In addition, Section 241(b)(9) allows the EAC to periodically study election administration issues, including methods of educating voters on all aspects voter participation.

To assist with collecting data, the EAC contracted Publius, a non-partisan non-profit organization to organize and conduct a voter information website design study and workgroup. This study is the aggregation of expert opinion at the time the study was conducted. It is ultimately exploratory in nature. The recommendations contained herein outline the current development, function and usefulness of voter information websites.

As election officials define, refine, design and utilize the recommendations to build and maintain voter information websites a more accurate sense of the utility of the recommendations presented and uncovered in this study. Field experience, combined with these initial reference recommendations, and the emergence of controls should result in the possibility of a more quantitative study in the future.

At some point, the time will come to revisit voter information website design and see how well these recommendations hold up.

Overview

Preliminary research was conducted online and over the phone. Findings were compiled and presented to a panel of experts to spark comment and discussion. The resulting expert opinion was reviewed and compiled to produce the recommendations in this document.

Online Research

In November 2005, the EAC began a comprehensive survey of voter information websites. This study reviewed hundreds of election information websites from various jurisdictions across the county. Seventy-one voter information websites[21] chosen for detailed study at a minimum could answer the question: "Am I registered to vote?" This distinction meant that the site itself had to be able to reference a voter registration file in order to qualify for in-depth study.

From November 2005 through February 2006 the selected voter information websites were reviewed and documented in three stages:

A thorough examination of information available online was categorized and distilled as discrete answers to anticipated voter questions. These anticipated questions were categorized in order to extrapolate the answer to the question: "What questions did the author of this website antici-pate answering?" This extrapolated data was averaged across the studied websites and a distinct pattern emerged that substantiated the initial survey research: "Am I registered to vote?" and "Where do I vote?" were found to be the two most anticipated questions from voters.

New vectors were introduced to the aggregate data, focusing on the websites that offered the most detailed information and those that had been in existence the longest. The goal was to see what features may have been anticipated and which features had been added as service ex-panded. Many of these features indicated that newer full-featured websites are already building on the functionality of more established sites. Features of these more robust sites were categorized and averaged, and the most common question extrapolated from feature-rich websites was: "What is on the ballot?"[22]

Finally, information delivery methods were categorized and averaged to understand how the information was delivered, and extrapolate what concerns were considered in the develop-ment of the delivery method. Categories were developed and delivery methodologies cataloged, which resulted in the detailed study of privacy discussed in this document.

Phone Interviews

The study then conducted follow-up phone interviews with the election administrators re-sponsible for the websites identified above to gather further data about the policy and political motivations and execution of these projects. Administrators were asked a variety of questions, such as:

- How did your project come into being?
- Was it done in house?
- What were the obstacles you encountered in setting up your site?
- What went right?
- What would you do differently?
- Do you have future plans for changing or expanding the site?
- How much did it cost to create the site?
- How popular is your site with your constituency?
- Many interviewees were asked other follow-up questions as new issues emerged.

As part of the study, the contractor requested detailed website log-file information. However, few of the sites in the study could furnish log-file data, resulting in too few data to generate an accurate sample.

General Development Path

Phone interviews with the administrators who were responsible for the voter information on their websites revealed that there was no uniform path to voter information website development. Some election jurisdictions developed their websites through supplementary riders to their voter registration database development contracts. Some projects also started as add-on functionality to a voter registration file that displayed more information than is recommended in this study. Some of the most user-friendly voter information websites were done in-house, as were some of the most unwieldy ones. Some election jurisdictions contracted out the development of their websites while others hired consultants to assist in development, assessing user experiences and marketing.

Project Conclusion

From April to June 2006, additional websites, many newly created for the 2006 midterm election, were reviewed and added to the study. All 50 state election websites were reviewed for changes at this time.

On June 27, 2006, the EAC hosted the voter information website design workgroup of technology experts, election administrators, advocacy organizations and other stakeholders. Participants were presented with the results of the second research study. A number of discussions that focused on voter education and website design resulted from that meeting and the research study. Feedback and recommendations from that meeting have been documented and are cited throughout this best practices document.

EAC Project Team

Edgardo Cortés, Election Assistance Commission
Karen Lynn-Dyson, Election Assistance Commission
Tamar Nedzar, Election Assistance Commission

Publius Project Team

Vincent M. Keenan, *Primary Investigator, Author*
Rebecca Houtman, *Writer, Editor*
Liese Hull, *Writer, Editor*

Additional Writers, Researchers, and Contributors

Kenneth Paulus, *Publius*
Alan Gutierrez, Think New Orleans

Conference Participants

Edgardo Cortés, *Election Assistance Commission*
Karen Lynn-Dyson, *Election Assistance Commission*
Tamar Nedzar, *Election Assistance Commission*
Vince Keenan, Director, *Publius, Voter Information Website Study Primary Investigator*
Kenneth Paulus, *Publius, Voter Information Website Conference Coordinator*
Sherif Abushadi, *Technical consultant*
Erika Aust, *Assistant Director, Office of the Secretary of State of Washington*
Mark Backus, *Network Security Engineer, CyberLogic Consulting*
Julia Bauler, *Office of the Secretary of State of Indiana*
Jo-Anne Chasnow, *Project Vote*
Maria Delvalle-Koch, *Division of Elections, State of New Jersey*
Kathleen Demers, *Institute of Politics, Harvard University*
Bobbie Egan, King County, Washington
Jennifer Faison
Alan Gutierrez, *Think New Orleans*
Russell Kasselman, *Office of the Secretary of State of Washington*
Tia Nelis, *Project Vote and University of Illinois-Chicago*
Andy Rivera, *Advancement Project*
Ari Schwartz, *Center for Democracy and Technology*

Cindy Southworth, *National Network to End Domestic Violence*
Cheryl O'Donnell, *National Field Director, National Network to End Domestic Violence*
Janice Winfrey, *City of Detroit, City Clerk*
David Tom, *Director of Elections, San Mateo County, California*

Additional Reviewing Experts

Doug Chapin, Pew Center on the States

From July through September 2006, results for the research study and the workgroup comments were reviewed and preliminary findings were developed for presentation to the EAC. On September 21, the preliminary findings were presented to the EAC at a public meeting in St. Louis.[23]

The best practices final report was compiled through October and November 2006, and revised in early 2007. Online comments from workgroup participants were solicited and a third review of all 50 state websites was also done at this time. EAC staff and Publius have worked together to edit the document for final release.

APPENDIX B. DEFINITIONS

Dynamic Data: Data that is tailored to the individual viewer based on the registration information supplied. For example, dynamically generated ballots make use of a voter's registration information to provide a list of contests exclusive to the individual voter.

Examples of dynamic data include: (1) registration status, (2) polling place location on interactive maps, (3) type of voting equipment specific to each polling place, (4) type of ballot used at a specific polling place, (5) initiatives and amendments specific to each ballot, and (6) calendars of upcoming elections.

Election Information Website: A website that provides information about elections and the election process.

Static Data: Information displays that are the same for each viewer. For example, static voter information websites display generic sample ballots that may or may not resemble the actual ballot voters will see on Election Day.

Examples of static data include: (1) how to apply for an absentee ballot, (2) election dates, (3) polling place hours of operation, (4) registration deadlines, (5) district maps and boundaries, (6) how to become a poll worker, and (7) instructions and/or frequently asked questions.

Voter Information Website: A website that provides information specific to an individual voter by referencing the current voter registration file. Voter information websites are distinct from election information websites in that they utilize public access to official voter registration records.

Voter Registration Look-up Mechanism: A utility that determines a voter's identity in order to display voter-specific registration information. Such a utility may require that the user enter identifying information; or information may be retrieved by drilling down through several menus.

Voters with Special Circumstances: Voters with special circumstances include voters who recently moved to a new jurisdiction, voters who have had their voting rights restored following a felony, deceased voters, and voters with limited reading comprehension.

APPENDIX C. INDEX OF EAC ADVISORIES IN THIS DOCUMENT

The following are the EAC Recommendations that were presented in this document. Following each recommendation is the page number where it can be found.

Preliminary Planning — Recommendations

3.1: Answer the question "Am I registered to vote?" (P.7)
3.2: Review legal considerations. (P.7)
3.3: Update voter records as often as possible. (P.7)
3.4: Adopt a neutral voice. (P.7)
3.5: Use effective design principles. (P.8) 3.6: Contract out work as needed. (P.8)
3.7: Review contractors' prior work. (P.8)
3.8: Consider commercial off-the-shelf (COTS) and open source solutions. (P.8)
3.9: Establish clear goals before development. (P.8)
3.10: Inventory data sources. (P.8)
3.11: Plan for high capacity peaks. (P.9)
3.12: Consider intellectual property and copyright issues. (P.9)
3.13: Document project development and system functionality. (P.9)
3.14: Budget for development, hosting, capacity, and promotion. (P.9)
3.15: Track usage patterns. (P.9)

Features – Recommendations

4.1: Provide voters with the answer to the question "Where do I vote?" (P.10)
4.2: Add map links to polling locations. (P.10)
4.3: Do not provide voters with driving directions. (P.10)
4.4: When including mapping programs, use the simplest versions available. (P.10)
4.5: Provide voters with a sample ballot. (P.11)
4.6: Display sample ballots exactly as they will appear on Election Day. (P.11)
4.7: Link sample ballots to helpful information. (P.11)
4.8: Do not link to incumbent government websites on a voter guide. (P.11)
4.9: Give voters the ability to track absentee ballots online. (P.11)

142 U.S. Election Assistance Commission

4.10: Allow users to check the status of provisional ballots online. (P.11)
4.11: Provide instructions for how to use voting equipment. (P.12)
4.12: Post Election Day times and polling location hours prominently. (P.12)
4.13: Provide other readily-available information neatly and in a logical manner. (P.12)

Marketing and Promotion – Recommendations

5.1: Consider different user audiences in promoting a voter information website. (P.13)
5.2: Repetition equals reinforcement. (P.13)
5.3: Use traditional media to promote voter information websites. (P.13)
5.4: Include your voter information website address on all voter outreach and election materials. (P.13)
5.5: Encourage election staff to direct voters to the voter information website. (P.14)
5.6: Adjust your capacity to account for your promotion. (P.14)
5.7: Identify and consider factors that may increase traffic. (P.14)
5.8: Make voter information website addresses simple and easy to remember. (P.14)
5.9: Build promotion around a single website address. (P.14)
5.10: Allow official voter information websites to be used as a tool for local voter outreach programs. (P.14)

Security and Privacy – Recommendations

6.1: Do not expose the official registry file to the Internet. *(official voter registry file security)* (P.15)
6.2: Do not expose data to the Internet that is not used by your voter information website. *(unused registry data security)* (P.16)
6.3: Avoid asking for too much information. *(online transaction security)*(P.16)
6.4: Review and comply with your jurisdiction's security policies on encrypting data. *(online transaction security)* (P.16)
6.5: Make sure you know who is working with your voter information. *(web development security and individual voter privacy)* (P.17)
6.6: Use increased security if you set out to vet the voter registry for accuracy, and avoid doing so at the expense of voter security. *(online transaction security and individual voter privacy)* (P.17)
6.7: Display as little information as possible about the voter - just enough to answer the voter's question. *(online transaction security and individual voter privacy)* (P.17)
6.8: Avoid disclosing a voter's birth date or current address. *(individual voter privacy and security)* (P.18)
6.9: Make sure your website is not a stalking tool. (P.18) (individual voter privacy and security)
6.10: Review you website to make sure it does not facilitate identity theft. *(individual voter privacy and security)*(P.18)
6.11: Make sure your website does not facilitate election fraud. *(election security)*(P.19)

6.12: Use implied information when possible. (individual voter privacy and transaction security)(P.19)

6.13: Avoid displaying information about more than one voter. *(individual voter privacy and transaction security)*(P.20)

6.14: Avoid using lists (individual voter privacy and transaction security) (P.20)

6.15: Avoid information over-exposure. (individual voter privacy) (P.20)

6.16: Avoid asking for obscure information. *(online transaction security)* (P.21)

Designing a Positive user Experience – Recommendations

7.1: Move users quickly from general to specific information. (P.22)

7.2: Employ industry standard graphic design principles and highlight the most popular features. (P.22)

7.3: Review design to ensure simplicity. (P.22)

7.4: Use broad and simple language; link to legal detail as necessary. (P.23)

7.5: Encourage voters with complex questions to contact election administrators. (P.23)

7.6: Use clear and consistent menus and icons. (P.23)

7.7: Use simple and recognizable visual language. (P.23)

7.8: Avoid excessive graphic design. (P.23)

7.9: Use "Frequently Asked Questions." (P.24)

7.10: Avoid asking voters for information that is not readily-available. (P.24)

Accessibility – Recommendations

8.1: Establish Section 508 as a minimum requirement for usability. (P.25)

8.2: Follow foreign language requirements for printed materials on the website. (P.25)

8.3: Ensure that content is written at a basic or intermediate literacy level. (P.25)

8.4: Ensure that website design encompasses users of below-average Internet literacy. (P.26)

8.5: Ensure compliance with new technologies when designing a voter information website. (P.26)

8.6: Use simple technologies. (P.26)

8.7: Display pages in printer-friendly formats. (P.26)

8.8: Indicate polling location accessibility information. (P. 26)

APPENDIX D. LIST OF WEBSITES REVIEWED IN THIS STUDY[24]

State	Jurisdiction	Website
Alabama	Mobile County	http://www.mobile-county.net/probate/
Arizona	Secretary of State	https://servicearizona.com/webapp/evoter/select_language.do
Arkansas	Secretary of State	https://www.voterviewar-nova.org/
Arkansas	Pulaski County	http://www.pulaskiclerk.com/
California	San Mateo County	http://www.shapethefuture.org/voters/defaultasp
California	Sacramento County	http://www.pollingplacelookupsaccounty.net/LookupPollingPlace_Sea rchByDOBaspx
Colorado	Adams County	http://webappscoadams.co.us/ElcPoll/VoterSearchcfm
Colorado	Boulder County	http://www.coboulder.co.us/webapps/voter_reg/promptfornamehtml
Colorado	El Paso County	http://carelpasoco.com/VoteRegQueryasp
Colorado	Larimer County	https://www.colarimer.co.us/elections/voter_inquirycfm
Colorado	Weld County	https://www.coweld.co.us/departments/clerkrecorder/voter_lookup/ind excfm
Connecticut	Southington County	http://registrarssouthington.org/voterlist/votersphp
Connecticut	Vernon County	http://www.vernonelections.org/voterlookupphp
Delaware	Secretary of State	https://registertovoteelectionsdelaware.gov/VoterRegistration/controlle r?TransName=VOTERREG_MAINMENU
District of Columbia	Secretary of State	http://www.dcboee.org/voterreg/vic_step1asp
Georgia	Secretary of State	http://www.sosstate.ga.us/cgi-bin/locatorasp
Illinois	City of Rockford	http://www.voterockford.com/voters/regStatusaspx
Illinois	DuPage County	http://cmsdupageelections.com/pagesasp?pageid=984
Illinois	Kane County	http://www.kanecountyelections.org/VoterInformation/VoterInfoasp
Illinois	Lake County	http://www.colake.il.us/cntyclk/elections/voterservices/regvoterasp
Illinois	Vermilion County	http://wwwcovermilionilus/ctyvoterRegasp
Illinois	Will County	https://www.willcountydata.com/voternewinquiry/voter_lookup_input htm
Illinois	City of Chicago	http://chicagoelections.com/voterinfo/defaultaspx
Illinois	Champaign County	https://www.champaigncountyclerk.com/elections/registration_statusht ml
Illinois	Cook County	http://www.voterinfonet.com/sub/am_i_registeredasp
Illinois	Madison County	http://app1comadison.il.us/CountyClerk/VoterPolling/VoterRegistratio ncfm
Indiana	Secretary of State	http://www.indianavoters.com/PublicSite/Public/PublicVoterRegistrati onaspx?AspxAutoDetectCookieSupport=1

Voter Information Websites Study

(Continued)

State	Jurisdiction	Website
Kansas	Secretary of State	https://myvoteinfovoteks.org
Kansas	Johnson County	http://voterjocoelection.org/searchaspx
Kentucky	Secretary of State	https://cdcbpky.gov/VICWeb/indexjsp
Louisiana	Secretary of State	http://soslouisiana.gov/polllocator
Maine	Secretary of State	http://www.maine.gov/sos/cec/elec/votreghtm
Maine	City of Portland	http://www.portlandmaine.gov/voter/voterlookasp
Maryland	Secretary of State	http://mdelectionsumbc.edu/voter_registration/v2/vote_prodphp
Massachusetts	City of Boston	http://www.cityofboston.gov/elections/voter/
Michigan	Secretary of State	https://www.michigan.gov/vote
Michigan	Detroit	http://detroitvoterinfo
Michigan	Statewide Non-Governmental	http://www.publius.org
Missouri	Kansas City	http://www.kceb.org/electioninfo/electioninfophp
Montana	Yellowstone	https://securecoyellowstone.mt.us/elections/secure/rvoterinfoasp
Nebraska	Secretary of State	https://www.voterchecknecvrne.gov/
Nevada	Clark County	http://www.accessclarkcounty.com/election/homeasp
Nevada	Washoe County	http://www.cowashoe.nv.us/voters/regsearchphp
North Carolina	Secretary of State	http://www.sboestatenc.us/votersearch/seimsvothtm
North Dakota	Secretary of State	http://www.nd.gov/sos/forms/pdf/voteregpdf
Ohio	Secretary of State	http://www.sosstate.oh.us/sosapps/elections/voterqueryaspx
Ohio	Butler County	http://www.butlercountyelections.org/indexcfm?page=voterSearch
Ohio	Hancock County	http://6619413288/searchaspx
Ohio	Warren County	http://www.cowarren.oh.us/bdelec/search/where_to_vote/indexhtm
Ohio	Wood County	http://www.cowood.oh.us/boe/VoterSearchhtm
Ohio	Franklin County	http://www.cofranklin.oh.us/boe/apps/voter/indexasp
Ohio	Hamilton County	http://www.hamilton-co.org/BOE/votersearchsasp
Pennsylvania	Secretary of State	http://www.dosstate.pa.us/voting/cwp/viewasp?a=1206&Q=446253
Pennsylvania	Allegheny County	http://www.countyallegheny.pa.us/votedistricts/
Rhode Island	Secretary of State	http://www.secstate.ri.us/vic/
South Carolina	Secretary of State	https://webprodciosc.gov/SCSECVoterWeb/voterInformationSearch do

146 U.S. Election Assistance Commission

(Continued)

State	Jurisdiction	Website
Tennessee	City of Memphis	http://www.shelbynet.com/wconnect/vhistfile.htm
Texas	Montgomery County	http://www.comontgomery.tx.us/election/vrlookupasp
Texas	Collin County	http://www.collincountytexas.gov/elections/voter_registration/voter_registration_card_voterjsp
Texas	Dallas County	http://dalcoelections.org/votersasp
Texas	Denton County	http://electionsdentoncounty.com/goasp?Dept=82&Link=292
Texas	Fort Bend County	http://votecofort-bend.tx.us/WebVoter/defaultasp
Texas	Harris County	http://www.harrisvotes.org/non_frames/geninfohtm
Texas	Midland County	http://www.comidland.tx.us/elections/VoterDatabase/inputasp
Texas	Nueces County	http://www.conueces.tx.us/countyclerk/elections/search/
Texas	Tarrant County	http://inettarrantcounty.com:8010/ElectionCGI/gac1fw1p
Texas	Travis County	http://www.traviscountytax.org/showVoterSearchdo
Utah	Utah County	http://www.coutah.ut.us/Dept/ClerkAud/Elections/VoterSearchasp
Utah	Davis County	http://www.daviscountyutah.gov/clerkauditor/elections/registered_voter_search/registered_voter_searchcfm
Virginia	State Board of Elections	http://www.sbevirginia.gov/cms/Voter_Information/Where_Do_I_Vote/Polling_Place_Lookup_requestasp
Washington	Secretary of State	https://www.secstatewa.gov/elections/lookupaspx
Washington	King County	https://www.metrokc.gov/elections/pollingplace/voterlookupaspx
Washington	Whatcom County	http://wwww.hatcomcounty.us/auditor/election_division/general_information/voter_lookup/IE6/Indexasp
Washington	Statewide Non-Governmental	http://www.soundpolitics.com/voterlookuphtml
West Virginia	Secretary of State	http://www.wvvotes.com/voters/am-i-registeredphp

End Notes

[1] "Voting in Memphis", (www.shelbynet.com/voting - organization's main page, www.shelbynet.com/wconnect/vhistfile.htm - voter registration look-up page) was launched to check voter registration in three Tennessee counties against death records (SSID confirmation).

[2] "Sound Politics", (www.soundpolitics.com - organization's main page, www.soundpolitics.com/voterlookup.html - voter registration look-up page) was launched with the intention of monitoring reported inaccuracies in King County voter registration.

[3] For purposes of this study, the question: "Who won?" was excluded because it does not require tying results to a voter registration lookup utility.

[4] This section assumes that the voter information website's primary audience will be individual voters.

[5] City of Chicago website (prior to November 2006 revision).

[6] *Example of cost accounting challenges:* CanIvote.org sponsored by the National Association of Secretaries of State was widely reported at cost of under $10,000, but the actual cost accounting for the functionality of an aggregated website like CanIvote.org requires acknowledgement of the costs of the systems that actually provide the functionality. Although CanIVote.org can be advertised as "being able to provide registration information," its cost is the cost of creating a site that links to that service, not the service itself.

[7] See Appendix D for a list of websites reviewed in this study.

[8] This section assumes that websites will reference an online voter registration file to answer the question, "Am I registered to vote?"

[9] Such as Google Maps© and Yahoo Maps©

[10] www.publius.org (1996-present)

[11] Macomb County, MI: http://itasw0aep001.macombcountymi.gov/ AbsenteeBallot/faces/SearchAbsentee. jspx

[12] State of Indiana: http://www.indianavoters.com/PublicSite/Public/PublicProvisional.aspx

[13] "... while total usage in the United States is now at 71.1% of the population, among those in the 16-24 age group it is 90.8%." from the UCLA World Internet Project (2004) http://www.international.ucla.edu/bcir/research/article.asp?parentid=7488

[14] In this case, information that is perceived as "personal" such as name address and birth date regardless or official public record status.

[15] A theoretical fake website could be an exact duplicate of the official site, but collects information a voter submits then indicate that "the database is unavailable please check back later." If the official government website asks for first name, last name, date of birth and zip code or unique voter ID (or middle name, address, social security number or driver's license number) up front, before demonstrating any functionality voters could submit significant personal information before, if ever, they discover a scam.

[16] "We have taken the approach that [information available online to the public] is for the functionality of what you need to do to vote." (David Tom, San Mateo County - June 2006 EAC Working Group meeting)

[17] As in the "Safe at Home" Address Confidentiality Program employed by several states

[18] Fighting Back Against Identity Theft, US Federal Trade Commission: www.ftc.gov/bcp/edu/microsites/ idtheft/consumers/about-identity-theft.html#Howdothievesstealanidentity

[19] Fighting Back Against Identity Theft, US Federal Trade Commission: www.ftc.gov/bcp/edu/microsites/ idtheft/consumers/pretexting.html

[20] The National Assessment of Adult Literacy (NAAL) http://nces.ed.gov/Pubs2007/2007480.pdf

[21] Listed in Appendix D.

[22] Publius, Washington State, King County Washington, Johnson County Kansas

[23] http://www.eac.gov/Public_Meeting_092106.asp

[24] Websites reviewed in this study were active as of the study dates: October 2005 through April 2007.

INDEX

A

abuse, 129
access, 10, 16, 18, 28, 39, 42, 60, 64, 66, 69, 70,
    75, 76, 85, 89, 90, 92, 103, 104, 105, 108, 114,
    115, 116, 117, 119, 122, 123, 126, 128, 129,
    130, 132, 133, 134, 135, 136, 140
accessibility, 3, 43, 71, 91, 99, 113, 134, 136, 143
accounting, 28, 146
ADA, 33, 36, 62
administrators, 15, 16, 18, 23, 32, 34, 39, 59, 113,
    115, 116, 117, 118, 119, 120, 123, 124, 125,
    127, 132, 133, 134, 138, 143
adults, 135
advocacy, 116, 138
age, 12, 13, 14, 61, 125, 147
agencies, 12, 15, 65, 134
aggregation, 32, 136
Americans with Disabilities Act, 33, 62
appropriate technology, 36
assessment, 31
audit, vii, 1, 86, 105
authorities, 19, 130
authority, 5, 17, 21, 30
awareness, 124

B

backlash, 46
bandwidth, 120
banking, 36
banks, 63, 64, 92
barriers, 12, 32
base, 49
base rate, 49
benefits, 3, 11, 12, 18, 32, 34, 36, 44, 58, 59

breakdown, 124
browser, 114, 133, 134, 135, 136
Bureau of Labor Statistics, 60
businesses, 12, 15, 16, 58

C

cables, 36
call centers, 67
campaigns, 116, 118, 124
candidates, 19, 20, 21, 22, 30, 31, 34, 48, 49, 50,
    51, 91, 95, 114, 117, 118, 122, 136
case study, 2, 3, 16, 17, 44
casting, 64, 69, 94
category a, 80
CEE, 51, 53, 54, 55, 56
cell phones, 69, 135
Census, 13, 61
challenges, 10, 15, 35, 45, 46, 113, 114, 136, 146
Chicago, 62, 139, 144, 146
cities, 48, 63, 67, 104
citizens, 33, 53, 59, 68, 76, 84, 92
City, 49, 62, 67, 83, 90, 91, 96, 131, 140, 144,
    145, 146
Civil War, 58
closure, 16
coercion, 28
commercial, 15, 53, 120, 141
communication, vii, 42, 63, 64, 65, 69, 70, 94,
    125
communities, 66
community, 46, 47, 49, 50, 90, 109, 113, 134
compatibility, 134, 135
compensation, 17
complexity, 114
compliance, 6, 30, 119, 120, 134, 135, 143
computer, 29, 36, 70, 77, 87, 88, 90, 104, 134,
    136

computer systems, 36
Congress, 51, 56, 57
connectivity, 4, 7, 10
consciousness, 126
consensus, 15
consent, 110
Constitution, 30, 57, 62
consumers, 147
consumption, 127
contingency, 35, 37, 42, 43
conversations, 76
cooperation, 25
Copyright, 120, 141
cost, 6, 12, 16, 18, 19, 23, 35, 36, 43, 44, 45, 48, 49, 51, 55, 58, 69, 83, 84, 102, 119, 121, 138, 146
cost accounting, 146
counsel, 119
Court of Appeals, 10
criminal activity, 91, 129
culture, 39, 58
customer service, 69, 84, 85
customers, vii, 63
cycles, 2, 8, 32, 37, 39, 50, 127

D

data collection, 121
database, vii, 28, 75, 76, 77, 86, 91, 92, 103, 104, 105, 114, 118, 126, 127, 133, 136, 138, 147
democracy, 57
denial, 126
denial of service attack, 126
Department of Education, 135
Department of Health and Human Services, 132
Department of Justice, 10, 36, 62
Department of Labor, 53
deposits, 39
depth, 113, 137
direct cost, 6
direct costs, 6
directors, 65
disability, 123, 126
disclosure, 129, 131
discomfort, 134
disposition, 106
distribution, 4, 6, 10, 28, 32, 80, 91, 124, 126
District of Columbia, 13, 57, 65, 92, 110, 144
diversity, 64
DOJ, 62

E

economies of scale, 33, 35, 59
education, 23, 35, 113, 136, 138
election fraud, 142
e-mail, 65, 69, 94
emergency, 7, 21
empirical studies, 3
employees, 6, 12, 16, 17, 18, 37, 44, 48, 58
employment, 52
encouragement, 84
encryption, 127
endorsements, 118
engineering, 129
environment, 3
equality, 6
equipment, 6, 22, 36, 37, 43, 69, 91, 114, 117, 118, 123, 134, 140, 142
EST, 56, 57
evidence, 3, 7, 19, 28, 46, 59, 114
evolution, 2
execution, 138
exposure, 126, 130, 143

F

family life, 12
family members, 28
fear, 126
federal agency, 134
Federal funds, vii, 1, 91
Federal Government, 60
federal law, 110
financial, 35, 129
financial records, 129
flexibility, 7, 11, 21, 125
force, 30
foreign aid, 53
foreign language, 73, 135, 143
formula, 5, 34
fraud, 28, 31, 64, 71, 72, 74, 91, 99, 100, 126, 130
freedom, 69
funding, 4

G

general election, 1, 2, 5, 6, 8, 15, 17, 18, 20, 21, 22, 23, 24, 26, 34, 42, 47, 48, 49, 50, 54, 55, 56, 61
Georgia, 69, 144
get-out-the-vote, 37

Index

government expenditure, 24
governments, 58, 136
grouping, 80
guidelines, 113, 120, 121

H

handwriting, 26
HAVA, vii, 1, 56, 71, 99, 118, 123, 136
Hawaii, 11, 13, 14
Help America Vote Act, vii, 1, 29, 72, 110, 113, 136
high school, 17, 37
hiring, 6, 42, 50, 82, 120
history, 2, 19, 59, 61, 117
homes, 54, 69
host, 48, 121
House, 3, 4, 15, 23, 56, 57, 60, 82, 85, 86
House of Representatives, 4, 56, 57, 60
hypothesis, 43, 46

I

ideal, 15, 43
identification, 25, 26, 38, 56, 122, 132
identity, 25, 88, 108, 126, 127, 128, 129, 130, 131, 141, 142, 147
impairments, 29
incumbents, 123
individuals, 7, 11, 12, 13, 23, 28, 29, 30, 33, 39, 47, 52, 53, 54, 55, 56, 57, 58, 59, 129
industries, 133
industry, 119, 133, 143
information exchange, 126
information technology, vii, 114
integration, 76
integrity, 46, 53, 57, 59, 126, 128, 129
intellectual property, 120, 141
interface, 7, 69, 120, 132, 133
intimidation, 28, 31
issues, 2, 26, 32, 35, 37, 39, 42, 64, 67, 72, 74, 113, 114, 120, 124, 136, 138, 141

J

jurisdiction, vii, 2, 7, 16, 17, 21, 47, 53, 58, 59, 65, 67, 68, 70, 71, 83, 84, 85, 86, 89, 90, 92, 97, 101, 102, 104, 105, 109, 114, 119, 120, 123, 124, 125, 130, 131, 141, 142

L

languages, 100
laws, 10, 17, 22, 28, 71, 72, 73, 99, 119, 120, 133, 135
lead, 4, 46, 119
leadership, 94
legislation, 2, 4, 5, 20, 21, 22, 23, 44, 56, 91
leisure, 46
leisure time, 46
lens, 128
literacy, 118, 134, 135, 143
local government, 15, 18, 36
logistics, 33
Louisiana, 11, 13, 14, 44, 45, 47, 48, 62, 145

M

machinery, 28
majority, 24, 31, 66, 69, 73, 75, 76, 78, 79, 82, 84, 85, 88
management, 7, 36, 75, 76, 103, 104
Mandarin, 90
mapping, 117, 122, 141
marketing, 138
Maryland, 11, 12, 13, 14, 16, 17, 18, 145
mass, 25
materials, 32, 55, 73, 85, 110, 124, 135, 142, 143
matter, 96, 127
measurement, 51
media, 35, 56, 91, 116, 124, 142
median, 64, 68, 80, 86, 87
medical, 54
messages, 69, 117
Microsoft, 117
Microsoft Word, 117
military, 71, 123
minority groups, 10
Missouri, 145
models, 125
Montana, 11, 13, 14, 17, 145

N

negative consequences, 32
neutral, 6, 119, 141
next generation, 94

O

obstacles, 132, 138

officials, vii, 1, 3, 4, 6, 7, 8, 10, 11, 12, 15, 16, 17, 18, 19, 21, 23, 24, 25, 26, 28, 29, 30, 32, 33, 34, 35, 37, 39, 42, 44, 46, 47, 48, 49, 50, 51, 52, 53, 54, 55, 57, 58, 59, 63, 64, 65, 66, 69, 70, 91, 92, 114, 115, 124, 137

operating system, 133

operations, vii, 22, 36, 54, 86, 114

opt out, 75

organize, 136

outreach, 69, 90, 109, 118, 124, 125, 142

outreach programs, 125, 142

outsourcing, 82, 86

oversight, 32

overtime, 12, 16, 44, 46, 49

ownership, 125

P

Pacific, 57

pairing, 115

parallel, 36, 133

participants, 140

password, 89, 96, 108

payroll, 6, 12

permission, iv, 134

personnel costs, 86, 105

persons with disabilities, 134

Philadelphia, 62

playing, 87, 108

police, 52, 53

policy, 120, 138

policymakers, 32

political parties, 34, 55

political party, 30, 31, 51, 96

polling, 1, 2, 5, 11, 12, 15, 17, 18, 19, 20, 23, 28, 31, 32, 33, 35, 36, 39, 43, 44, 46, 47, 48, 49, 50, 52, 53, 54, 55, 56, 57, 58, 59, 60, 64, 69, 71, 72, 73, 75, 76, 90, 91, 92, 94, 99, 106, 109, 114, 117, 118, 121, 122, 123, 126, 129, 130, 131, 136, 140, 141, 142, 143

population, 4, 6, 12, 13, 14, 56, 58, 61, 64, 68, 69, 123, 125, 147

population density, 58

potential benefits, 44

preparation, 24, 33

President, 12, 52

principles, 119, 124, 133, 141, 143

prisoners, 53, 54

professionals, vii, 114

profit, 136

programming, 90, 120

project, 35, 66, 110, 118, 120, 128, 138, 141

protection, 3

public education, 4

public service, 124

Puerto Rico, 2, 51, 52, 53, 54, 55, 56, 60, 65, 92

Q

quality of service, 119

query, vii, 62, 114, 131

questionnaire, 132

R

race, 51, 56

radio, 55, 124, 125

ramp, 136

reading, 133, 141

reading comprehension, 133, 141

real time, 86, 104, 105

reasoning, 11, 84

recall, 125, 132

recommendations, iv, 114, 136, 137, 139

recreation, 39

recruiting, 19, 47, 50, 55, 59, 72, 73, 99

reforms, 43

Registry, 126, 128

Rehabilitation Act, 134

reinforcement, 124, 142

relevance, 114

rent, 46, 49, 55

requirements, vii, 1, 4, 6, 10, 23, 52, 60, 90, 110, 134, 135, 143

researchers, 11, 12, 13, 15, 16, 39, 44, 66, 110

reserves, 57

resolution, 91

resources, 21, 33, 34, 42, 54, 72, 119, 120, 123, 125, 127, 134, 135

response, 43, 65, 66, 97, 109, 111, 134

response time, 134

revenue, 23

rights, 53, 141

risk, 122, 127

role playing, 87

rules, 5, 10, 21, 61, 119

S

safety, 128

school, 12, 15, 17, 18, 33, 48, 121, 126, 128

scripts, 78

second language, 135

Index

security, 15, 16, 18, 24, 36, 46, 58, 88, 89, 108, 119, 126, 127, 128, 129, 130, 131, 132, 142, 143

Senate, 4, 23, 30, 34, 44, 56, 61

sensitivity, 130

servers, 36

service provider, 82, 83, 85, 86, 102, 103, 107

services, 22, 64, 65, 69, 72, 76, 83, 91, 92, 96, 97, 98, 102, 104, 122, 124

shoots, 124

shortage, 42

showing, 2, 124

side effects, 57

signs, 4, 20, 38, 53

Social Security, 88, 108, 147

society, 44, 59

software, vii, 43, 78, 103, 114, 133, 134, 135, 136

solution, 57, 123

Spring, 11, 20

staff members, 46

staffing, 86, 87, 107

stakeholders, vii, 63, 138

state, 22, 23, 61, 83, 88, 91, 97, 100, 104, 114, 120, 121, 122, 125, 134, 135, 138, 140

states, 62, 92, 97, 118, 125, 128, 129, 147

statewide elections, 19, 26

statistics, 3, 54

statutes, 61

statutory foundation, 10

statutory provisions, 21

structure, 56

style, 29, 38, 53, 117

supervision, 21, 22, 26, 56

supervisor, 37

supervisors, 6

Supreme Court, 30, 52

surplus, 36

T

target, 118, 126, 129

teachers, 47

techniques, 64, 69

technologies, vii, 114, 134, 135, 143

technology, 4, 7, 29, 35, 36, 37, 42, 64, 74, 83, 100, 113, 136, 138

telecommunications, 73, 83

telephone, vii, 29, 63, 64, 67, 73, 90

telephones, 67

testing, 37, 43, 133, 135

text messaging, 64

theft, 126, 128, 129, 142, 147

threats, 126, 129

time periods, 31

total costs, 105

tracks, 34, 79

training, vii, 19, 33, 36, 37, 55, 63, 69, 73, 85, 88, 90, 91, 92, 99, 118

translation, 135

transport, 6, 24, 53, 55

transportation, 6, 32

troubleshooting, 73, 99

turnout, 3, 6, 7, 8, 10, 11, 13, 14, 16, 17, 18, 19, 20, 22, 23, 26, 29, 30, 31, 32, 34, 36, 39, 42, 43, 44, 45, 48, 49, 50, 51, 55, 58, 59, 60, 61, 95

U

U.S. Department of Commerce, 61

U.S. Department of Labor, 60

uniform, vii, 1, 5, 10, 56, 57, 138

United, 1, 13, 14, 18, 30, 52, 56, 60, 61, 62, 63, 66, 134, 147

United States, 1, 13, 14, 18, 30, 52, 56, 60, 61, 62, 63, 66, 134, 147

updating, 86, 105

urban, 22, 109

urban renewal, 22

V

validation, 26, 28

variables, 89, 108

variations, 48, 134

vehicles, 55

vein, 67

victims, 129

videos, 123

vision, 29

vote, 1, 2, 3, 7, 8, 12, 19, 20, 21, 22, 23, 24, 25, 26, 28, 29, 30, 31, 32, 33, 34, 35, 36, 37, 38, 39, 42, 43, 44, 50, 52, 53, 54, 55, 56, 57, 58, 59, 61, 62, 64, 67, 74, 84, 88, 91, 95, 100, 114, 115, 116, 117, 118, 119, 121, 125, 130, 136, 137, 141, 145, 147

voting, vii, 1, 2, 3, 4, 5, 6, 7, 8, 9, 10, 11, 12, 13, 14, 19, 21, 22, 23, 24, 25, 26, 28, 29, 30, 31, 32, 33, 34, 35, 36, 37, 38, 39, 42, 43, 44, 45, 46, 47, 48, 49, 50, 51, 52, 53, 54, 55, 56, 57, 58, 59, 60, 61, 64, 68, 69, 70, 71, 72, 73, 85, 91, 94, 98, 99, 108, 114, 115, 117, 118, 123, 125, 126, 140, 141, 142, 145, 146

Voting Rights Act, 10

W

Washington, 16, 57, 60, 61, 62, 111, 139, 146, 147
wealth, 132
web, 117, 119, 126, 127, 128, 142
web pages, 117
websites, vii, 113, 114, 115, 116, 117, 118, 119, 120, 121, 122, 123, 124, 125, 126, 128, 132, 133, 134, 135, 136, 137, 138, 140, 141, 142, 146, 147
wires, 37

Wisconsin, 68
workers, 6, 12, 16, 17, 18, 19, 32, 33, 34, 35, 37, 39, 44, 47, 48, 50, 54, 55, 58, 59, 63, 66, 67, 72, 73, 90, 91
workforce, 46, 47
workload, 37
workstation, 104
worldwide, 36

Y

yield, 7